Layman Irish Catholic

Letters of an Irish Catholic Layman

Layman Irish Catholic

Letters of an Irish Catholic Layman

ISBN/EAN: 9783744687430

Printed in Europe, USA, Canada, Australia, Japan

Cover: Foto ©Thomas Meinert / pixelio.de

More available books at **www.hansebooks.com**

LETTERS

OF AN

IRISH CATHOLIC LAYMAN

BEING AN EXAMINATION OF THE PRESENT STATE OF IRISH AFFAIRS IN RELATION TO THE IRISH CHURCH AND THE HOLY SEE.

(1883-4.)

SHOWING

That the Home Rule, Land, and Education Movements, with which the Irish people are identified, are in perfect conformity with natural justice and Catholic principles, and are in essence a struggle between a Christian and a non-Christian Civilisation.

SEVENTH THOUSAND. REVISED AND ENLARGED.

[REPRINTED FROM THE "NATION."]

PRINTED FOR AND PUBLISHED BY
J. J. LALOR, NORTH EARL STREET, DUBLIN;
AND SOLD BY
JOHN HEYWOOD, MANCHESTER ; CAMERON AND FERGUSON, GLASGOW ; AND
WILLIAMS AND BUTLAND, 47, WHITECHAPEL, LONDON.

Price One Shilling. Handsomely bound in Cloth, Two Shillings.

"I want an intelligent and well-instructed laity—a laity not arrogant, nor rash in speech, nor disputatious, but men who know their religion, who enter into it, who know just where they stand. I want you to rouse yourselves, to understand where you are, and to know yourselves. I would aim primarily at organisation, edification, cultivation of mind, growth of the reason. It is a moral force, not a material, which will vindicate your profession and secure your triumph."—*Cardinal Newman.*

"The great triumph of Satan is to produce a 'Liberal Catholic.' Such a man as Pius IX. lately proclaimed a worse enemy than a heretic or infidel. 'It is,' says Brownson, 'the liberalism which has penetrated the Catholic camp which renders Catholics throughout Europe so imbecile in defence of Catholic interests. . . . It is all the work of liberal Catholics, without whom Agnostics and infidels would be reduced to impotence.'"—*Tablet, 31st January, 1875.*

" A man's life-blood is frozen in its current, his intellect deadened, and his very soul annihilated by the everlasting dinning into his ears by the 'wise' and 'prudent,' more properly the timid and selfish, of the admonition to be politic, to take care not to compromise one's cause or one's friends. My soul revolted, and revolts even to-day, at this admonition. Almost the only blunders I ever committed were made when I studied to be politic, and prided myself on my diplomacy."—*O. A. Brownson.*

TO

THE IRISH PEOPLE

AT HOME AND ABROAD,

ARDENT PROFESSORS AND TRUE DEFENDERS OF THE FAITH,

BEST EXAMPLES OF ITS POWER

IN GUARDING PURITY OF MORALS,

INSPIRING THE SPIRIT OF SACRIFICE,

AND ENFORCING INVIOLABLE FIDELITY TO CONSCIENCE,

BEARING BEFORE THE WORLD FOR THREE CENTURIES

THE STANDARD OF THE CROSS,

AND BY IT TRIUMPHING,

THE FOLLOWING LETTERS,

ILLUSTRATING THEIR PRINCIPLES AND ADVOCATING THEIR RIGHTS,

ARE RESPECTFULLY INSCRIBED

BY

AN IRISH CATHOLIC LAYMAN.

January, 1884.

PREFACE.

THE argument running through the following pages may be usefully stated in almost self-evident propositions :—

1. That man, in virtue of his creation, is bound to certain duties and acquires certain rights.

2. Chief among these is the duty of conserving his existence and developing his being to the highest perfection his nature and conditions allow.

3. This includes (1st) right of defence, and (2nd) freedom to do all that in fulfilment of his duty nature and circumstances entitle him to do.

4. That these duties and rights in the individual of necessity attach to the family, which is the completion and perpetuation of the individual.

5. That in the order of God's providence mankind is divided into aggregations of families called nations, to each of which is assigned its geographical place and boundaries.

6. That these are distinguished by differences of origin, of characteristics, idiosyncrasies, feelings, and interests ; and that each has a natural right to develop its national life, and to seek its perfection and its end in its own way.

7. That one of these nations, marked by a national character and life of the most distinct and robust kind, has dwelt in Ireland from time immemorial.

8. That for centuries the common right of this people to live its own life in its own land has been denied it by a more powerful people, and that in the enforcing of this denial the stronger nation has committed against the weaker every crime of which humanity is capable.

9. That while the hostility of the stronger race has in later years been mitigated by the liberalising of ideas, the general softening of manners, and the growth of a more active and enlightened public opinion, it has never yet granted the slightest concession to any principle of justice, nor acquired any equitable right to govern, by seeking or desiring the welfare of the Irish people.

10. That the later connection of the two countries has been complicated and embittered by religious persecution. Sectarian malice on the side of the Government, and suffering for conscience sake on that of the people

have rendered the struggle rather as between Catholic and non-Catholic than as between England and Ireland.

11. That when Emancipation gave the Irish people power to organise and combine, they could, by using the means at their command, at any time have compelled the granting of every measure they were entitled to ask.

12. That such combination and organisation were, for many years, impossible by reason of the unworthiness of the Catholic aristocracy and gentry—their natural leaders.

13. That when the people have for good and all pushed these aside, and have combined and organised themselves with such astonishing results, their progress is retarded, their final triumph delayed, their very existence as a Catholic nation menaced by the unnatural, "stone-blind," suicidal alliance of a section of the Catholic Hierarchy with their avowed enemies ; and—

14. That this alliance bears its condemnation on its front by its betrayal of every Irish and Catholic interest. It violates Catholic principles in education. It contravenes the spirit of the Church in taking sides with the rich against the poor, with the proud against the humble, with the strong against the weak, with lawless tyranny against helpless innocence, with class privilege and sectarian ascendancy against popular freedom ; and in doing all this it supports a power showing in all its actions every evidence of diabolic inspiration.

The conclusion naturally flowing from these premises is this : That while the Irish people will go on, as they have every natural and Divine right to do, to conquer the freedom to live in their own way in their own country, the Castle ecclesiastic who has abandoned and opposed them, who in the hour of supreme struggle has taken sides with the enemy, will have in the new Ireland rapidly being made a very different position from that which he held in the old. At best he may find, as the French ecclesiastic of to-day, his ministrations accepted, but himself extruded from the social movements and political life of a country where he might have enjoyed the fulness of his proper influence and authority.

Whatever effect these letters may have in urging those who have the power to exert it in preventing the decay of the Catholic feeling of our people—to whatever extent they may help to introduce into Irish affairs a more disinterested, intelligent, and courageous Catholic spirit—the greater part, if not the whole, of the merit is due to the proprietor of the *Nation.* No other man in Ireland would have dared to print them, and

in no other journal could they have properly appeared; for the
Nation has ever been, under its present direction, as Catholic
as Irish, and as Irish as Catholic. Nothing has more amazed the writer
than the deep and widespread interest they have excited. They have
travelled far on special journeys, and in more than one instance under
distinguished auspices—to the States and Canada, to far California, to
farther Australia—and from every place without one exception has
come back assurance of interest and sympathy. It may not be
presumptuous to hope that they may even penetrate to Rome itself, and
perchance give the Sacred College some more reliable ideas about Irish
persons and things than they have been receiving from the Castle bishop
and the emissaries of the English Government, who must necessarily
be slanderers of the Irish people.

Treating respectfully—at least in intention—but with very uncommon
freedom, of the policy and action of ecclesiastics of high rank, they have
been received by other ecclesiastics with a remarkable warmth of
approval. This is not due to any newness of matter or merit of
treatment. Desultory and fragmentary from the circumstances of their
composition, wanting in close-knit argument and logical evolution, they
are so far from the ideal projected in the writer's mind that he is more
inclined to apologise for forestalling the work of some more competent
hand than to accept praise for its execution. What is most strongly
present to him is this : that if one of our literary chiefs—a Sullivan
or a Duffy—had undertaken the task, he might have struck such a
smashing blow at Irish ecclesiastical Whiggery as would have swept it
out of sight for ever. One merit the letters may claim, they photograph
(as regards the subjects they embrace) the mind of Catholic Ireland, and
of Irish Catholics everywhere. They give articulate expression to thoughts
and feelings which are powerfully moving a million of hearts. They say
what multitudes of people desire to say, and which many could say far
better, but are prevented from saying at all, and they are made to do
this under the conviction that it is better to give those thoughts and
feelings voice than to allow them to rankle and inflame till they issue in
deadly injury to the Church.

One only criticism of any weight has reached me. It is from an
English layman ; and it goes to point out that, however true the letters
may be, there is a radical incongruity in the situation. · One cannot, he
says, teach one's teacher, or rule one's ruler ; while the public criticism
of prelates by name shocks his feelings as a Catholic. And with my

friend so far I entirely agree.   It is incongruous, anomalous, abnormal, but so is the state of things which is the subject of discussion.   It is contrary to the practice proper to Catholics in ordinary circumstances, but so is the policy of the personages whose public action is criticised. In a word, the justification of the letters is in their *necessity*, and of that the writer has not permitted himself to be the judge.   He has accepted a direction, not undertaken a responsibility.

Though the letters were begun on the spur of a great anxiety, it must not be supposed that they are mere hasty or shallow thoughts strung together without consideration.   They are, in truth, the outcome of an observation of society in the three kingdoms at once so minute and so general as to be necessarily rare, of information drawn from most varied sources, and of long reflection on the two truths which the writer takes to lie at the very root, or rather to form the foundation of, all true and healthy civilisation—the one, that "Godliness is profitable;" the other, "Seek ye first the kingdom of God and his justice, and all things shall be added unto you"—that is, that to the individual or the people seeking before all their spiritual good, such measure of temporal prosperity and happiness is added, under ordinary conditions, as the wisdom of God sees to be consistent therewith.   The tracing of the laws which always and everywhere operate in society results in proving to demonstration the truth of these texts.   Well would it be for the empire if some master-hand were employed in showing to the practical English people the one only way by which the pauperism, misery, and crime, which now threaten to uproot their social state from its foundations, can be attacked and overcome.

They are not in the way of learning these truths or putting these laws into operation; for on two questions, the Irish and the Catholic, they seem incapable, in the general, of any right exercise of reason, or, indeed, of keeping within the bounds of sanity.   Assuming it to be historically true, as Cardinal Manning has frequently pointed out, that the English people did not apostatise, but were robbed of their faith, so well has the ceaseless stream of slander begun at the Reformation done its work, that no matter what causes led to the lamentable revolt, the English mind could not be more blind than it is to those things which make for its peace.   But suppose England ready to listen, there is no one in the Senate to speak.   There are in the Upper House many Catholic noblemen ; they might as well be dummies, for any mark they make in the order of Catholic ideas or interests. There are many Catholic members in the Lower House of a very different stamp; but up to this these men have had to struggle unceasingly for the barest elements of justice: the mere right to live on the part of the bulk of their constituents. There are members in the Commons eminently Catholic, but no Catholic party: nor can such be formed from the present elements. The Irish members will have, for some time to come, too much to do in other ways to undertake many of the duties which would properly fall to such a party; and for the present, at all events, its principal constituents must be looked for elsewhere. Though the feeling at present in Ireland is strongly—and, it must be confessed, justly— against again entrusting English Catholics with interests they have so frequently neglected or betrayed, I have the strongest conviction, founded on personal knowledge, that there are in that body several men who would render to the Irish cause inestimable service, and whose presence in the Irish Party would draw together the Catholics of the two nations, and do away with the exasperation now fostered by the anti-Irish Catholic faction in England. And this union would make for our interests, secular as well as religious. No matter where feeling or sentiment may lead us, we have to aim at the possible as well as the right. No man outside Bedlam—no one who is not either a fool or a "red"—contemplates separation. Against this, no matter how right in the abstract or defensible in theory, seven-eighths of the Catholics of Ireland and all the non-Catholics would join, while behind both would be the enormous Conservative force of the Church. The matter is not discussible, and may be relegated to debating societies, or anywhere out of the range of practical politics.

One thing, therefore, above all, should be in the minds of men of good will in both countries, namely, to bring about an intelligent, intimate cordial union. Spite of many appearances to the contrary, the groundwork is being laid. for this. Some English politicians and several members of the press have mastered the Irish question, and are leavening others with their knowledge. Little by little the aristocratic governing class is losing its hold; and this class forms the real, the greatest obstacle, to the union of the peoples, since that would sound the knell of their monopoly. At this moment the presence of half-a-dozen honest, sensible Englishmen in the Irish representation would hasten this union more than any other means, and gain for our arguments admittance and support in quarters they are now not so much as heard of. No prudent statesman, no great general, omits any precaution or any aid which can secure victory. And as it must be conceded that the welfare of the two countries goes for a practical unity of idea and aim—not the present hateful, unnatural union of force—the sooner we begin to prepare for this consummation, the sooner it will be reached.

More than once in the course of these letters I have been compelled, from certain points of view, to speak of the English people with great severity. It would be unfair to them and myself if these opinions were permitted to appear as a final or complete judgment. In such case they would be the reverse of exact. Nothing can be gained by disparaging your adversary unjustly. And any conclusion which denied to the English people some of the grandest qualities of human nature—a foremost place amongst the nations of the world—would be manifestly untrue.* Unhappily, their worst side has been always turned to us; and they are so misled by prejudice, and blinded by the malice of their enemies and ours, that they are for the most part rendered incapable of seeing the most obvious truth, or doing the commonest justice, when things Irish or Catholic are concerned. We want more intercourse of the friendly sort. Half a dozen men of the stamp of the late Frederick Lucas (it is impossible to keep him out of one's mind through all this long discussion) would do more, naturally and necessarily, to bring about a thorough understanding between the two countries than six times the number of Irish members, however able. And this end seems to the writer, save one other, the very noblest and best which can engage the attention or stimulate the action of our best citizens on either side. On our part it would be the truest policy, as well as the noblest revenge, not only to meet half-way all approaches to amity, but to use our better judgment and more generous and elevated views to hasten the approach of a perfect understanding.

* In the appendix will be found a masterly analysis of the English character which I adopt almost in its entirety.

PREFACE TO SECOND EDITION.

THE first issue (of several thousands) of this little book was exhausted in a few weeks, and after an interval of four years it is still continually called for.

I refrained from reprinting till now for two reasons—one, that I had the hope, not yet abandoned, of presenting an essay on the "Relations of the Church and the World," which should have more of scientific method and proportion, and therefore of permanent value. Travelling discursively over a practically illimitable field, the letters want that concentration and point so desirable in any work that aims at public enlightenment. And the other reason was a natural dislike to keep alive a discussion in which the names and actions of distinguished persons were somewhat roughly handled.

This demand for such a fugitive production is extraordinary, if not unprecedented; and one naturally looks for its cause. It must be sought not in the style or matter of the book itself—for in either, if there be any merit, there is nothing new—but in the crisis in which it appeared, and in the society to which it appealed. The simple statement of Catholic principles in respect of the constitution of the Church, and her duties and powers in the external order; the endeavour to show, in a manner however jejune and imperfect, the connection between the domination of the Christian idea and the progress and happiness of human society, were things so strange and unusual that they drew public attention as if they were discoveries, or at least things so out of the common as to have the character of originality. Not that the root of the matter was not inchoate in the public mind; the prompt and wide acceptance of the letters, both in premiss and conclusion, is evidence of that fact, and evidence also of the just claim of Ireland to be held profoundly and essentially Catholic. But it is proof also that Catholic ideas are so overlaid in our midst with others not Irish, but foreign and false, that when the former are presented in their logical order, as applied to public affairs, they have all the freshness and charm of novelty. The condition of mind in what are called educated circles—the current and aim of their intellectual life are not Catholic. And this must also be taken as a proof that our ecclesiastical chiefs have not been sufficiently awake to the fact that modern civilisation is apostate; and that what is called the modern spirit, of which we see sadly too much even in Catholic Ireland, is intensely hostile to Christianity.

From the Irish Church the Irish people had a right to demand that the bottom facts of their history and their struggle should be taught constantly and with authority. They did not get this teaching. On the contrary, for three-quarters of a century a considerable number of Irish bishops were apparently, themselves wanting in true knowledge of, and were and are openly or secretly hostile to, the popular claims ; and at this day I have absolute proof that no small number would still vote, if they could—if a vigilant public opinion did not constrain them—against their own and their people's best interests. Catholic emancipation was got in spite of them, for they were always willing to exchange open oppression, of late neither dangerous nor deadly, for the secret chain of the veto. Now, thanks to the "grace of God and the favour of the Apostolic see," united with the prayers and desires of the Irish people expressed in no hesitating fashion, we have a Metropolitan who is slowly drawing the Irish Church into line with the people. In our day no appointment more clearly Providential has been made in the Universal Church. The career of this great High Priest, since his occupation of the See of Dublin, the versatility, ability, and courage he has shown in defence of his nation, are at once the highest evidence of his fitness, and the strongest proof of the true nature of the policy followed by his predecessors for more than a century. I may venture to point to it also as a justification of the view taken in these letters of the public conduct of these venerable men.

We are dealing now with paramount interests—the very existence of the Irish Church and nation—and we must not hesitate to say that to the policy followed by a large proportion of Irish ecclesiastics (so large that it would be incredible in the absence of absolute proof) is answerable in the second place (the first of course being the foreign and hostile rule which is destroying us) for most of the evils we have suffered for half a century ; that numbers of these have been concussed into the present movement ; that they still retain their anti-Irish opinions, and would go Castlewards to-morrow if they had a chance. And clearly it cannot be otherwise. The political conversion of aged men is impossible without a miracle, and this we have no right to expect. The Castle bishop of yesterday is the Castle bishop of to-day, no matter how appearances vary. He is what he is, not for want of judgment or knowledge, but from want of heart ; and with age that vital organ of thought as well as feeling grows seared and dull. With age, also, the intellect gets as fixed and set as the body, and as incapable of renewal or transformation. Nearly all the chiefs of the Irish Church were born serfs; and the youth who saw the scourge wielded—who saw his father tremble before the bailiff or kneel to the agent*—thinks in his old age that it is a great thing to be permitted to live without fear.

Certain it is that the men of this evil past, no matter how personally excellent, are quite unfit to guide a vigorous nation within one hour of its final emancipation. The Irish people have always been in advance of the majority of the Irish Church, not only in public spirit, but I dare to say it, in Catholic feeling. Prudence would seem to dictate to the party which cannot range itself with the Irish people in their struggle for God's justice and truth, to carefully conceal its secret desires, lest a multitude of evils should follow their manifestation. But it is not so. The last example of the Castle Bishop is unhappily the most pronounced and the most dangerous. The appointment has one advantage, namely, that it shows what manner of man would get promotion under a veto ; the kind that would be made by English intrigue, and the favour of Irish Whig Catholic aristocrats, and that it puts beyond the possibility of repetition such another creation.

The necessity which dictated these letters, and which with their simple truthfulness has been held to be their justification, compels me to name the most Rev. Dr. Healy, coadjutor of Clonfert, as the latest and most unaccountable example of the Castle Bishop. This able prelate, to his honour, be it said, has risen from the humblest ranks. In his youth he touched in his own person the evils which sprung from English rule and Irish landlordism. He saw around him the hunger and cold and nakedness, bred of these diabolical agencies— the ignorance, the squalor, the misery of which they are the parents. And from these experiences he acquired the usual feeling of men of his class. He was a patriot while serving the curacies of Ballygar and Cliffony. It was only when he got to the neighbourhood of Dublin and was made free of Carton House that he saw in the Irish the outcome of the French revolution, and in the just claims of the Irish people to good government the overturning of society. There is want of candour in the use of the great revolution as a name of terror by certain enemies of the

---

* A common practice in Mayo up to a very few years ago.

B

people.   If they were honest they would tell the causes of that fearful
outbreak.   They would show them to have been bred in a corrupt court
by a selfish and vicious aristocracy, and a compliant and wordly body of
ecclesiastics, strongly tinged with Erastianism.   But the Court Bishop of
the Regency would too closely resemble the Castle Bishop of to-day to
make these historical truths suitable for the latter's purposes.   He has,
therefore, carefully avoided telling us that all the essential motors of the
French Revolution—the corruption and tyranny of the Government; tne
suffering and decay of the people; the weakness of a portion of the
Church—have been and are in active existence in Ireland during this
century.   He has not told this, for the people would be prompt to draw
from the facts conclusions which could only end in his ruin.

Of Dr. Healy's anti-Irish feeling he has given in public and private a
multitude of proofs.   I will here content myself with one so recent
and patent that it will suffice.   His name (nor those of the five
priests subject to his *quasi* immediate control) was not affixed to the
recent protest of the Diocese of Clonfert against the infamous Coercion
Act.   Now Dr. Healy may not say to Lord Salisbury: "Quite right
my lord—those Irish savages are no more worthy of the franchise than
Hottentots; they are a scandal to civilisation, a disgrace to humanity,
and your intended extermination of a million of them has my blessing."
The Bishop does not say it, but he acts as if he thought it, and his
Castle friends take heart of grace accordingly.   Now we dare not even
think that Dr. Healy is not honest in his change of view.   But what a
contempt for human reason does not this change suggest!   Here is a
Bishop, not born in slavery, nor fixed with old ideas, but young, of
conspicuous ability and strength of character, with all the light that
experience of the present struggle throws on the nature of the principles
involved—here, I say, is an Irish ecclesiastic deliberately entering Dublin
Castle, which he knows, or ought to know, is an antechamber of Hell,
and, in the sight of his outraged flock, making peace and alliance with
Antichrist seated therein.   Whatever be the Bishop's motive, by what
unaccountable process he has wiped out his earlier experience and blinded
his reason, one thing is clear—he has mistaken his day.*   Time was when

---

* When writing above I knew indeed that the Nemesis was inevitable, but did not
think it would come so quickly and so decisively as the following, extracted from the
Times, discloses :—
   " BOYCOTTING A ROMAN CATHOLIC BISHOP.—' Catholicus ' writes from Woodford on the 16th :
The Most Rev. Dr. Healy, Coadjutor Bishop of this diocese, is in this instance the victim against

he could have found his account in such a turning of his back on himself.
That time is no longer. He should take warning by the fate of Dr.
Scarisbrick, who conspired with the most detested tool of English tyranny,
Clifford Lloyd, against Sir J. P. Hennessy. He should well know that
when a Bishop has made void the faith and confidence of his people, the
Holy See is constrained, by its first duty—the salvation of souls—to make
other arrangements. He should ponder the words of the wise and able
Prelate of Meath : "Popularity in itself is in my eyes of no more value
than chaff. Popularity, as an aid in my work, I value exceedingly.
While I never courted popularity, I dread exceedingly unpopularity,
either with priests or people. I know that the Bishop who is not liked,
whose sympathies are not with his people, politically as well as religiously,
will fail in his work. . . . No matter what his ability, no matter what
his eloquence and zeal, all will be literally thrown away and his power
for the salvation of souls destroyed." Another prelate equally eminent
for patriotism and ability writes : "The influence of ecclesiastics over
the people *is* and *will be* in direct proportion with their real and practical
sympathy with their suffering flocks. When that is wanting there is
danger."

Much more could be said on this head which must remain for a
more convenient opportunity. I will content myself by quoting an
English writer* on the present movement—not at all as intending
it to have any individual application, but as showing how the West
British Irishman is viewed from the other side : "It is one of the
greatest honours you can pay a people to call them rebels when their

---

whom the League has employed its infamous and spiteful decrees. Wednesday and Thursday of
last week were the days appointed by his Lordship to hold confirmations at Cloncoe. It was
announced from the altar that it was his Lordship's wish that as many of the parishioners as
possible should attend on those days in order that he might address them. But what is the
result ? Two of the League's magnates busy themselves visiting the houses, warning the people
not to go, but to send 'the children to be confirmed, and none else.' . . . Why is all this ?
Because this distinguished prelate chooses to differ as to the plans and methods pursued by the
Leaguers, and is a staunch Unionist."

This occurrence at Cloncoe, and a similar threatened a short time since at a
neighbouring parish, could be foretold with perfect certainty. Dr. Healy would state
for his people principles true in the abstract, and reason from these in a way strictly
logical to show that the Irish movement is destructive of society, &c., &c. But his
people, by a truer method, see for certain that his specious syllogisms issue in their
ruin, and their sense of justice and of right is more than a match for his logic. This
is the way in which he has made an end of his authority, of all his power for good,
and by consequence of his right to reign in Clonfert ; and this is what has brought
into contempt what is called by his class "scientific theology." Correct it may be in
statement, utterly false and detestable it usually is in application and conclusion.

* Mr. Reid.

Government is alien and oppressive : while the most odious name you can give them in such circumstances is 'Loyalists.' I can conceive no creature to be a more loathsome leper than he who, sitting in the midst of such a history as that of Ireland—wet with blood—while hovering over him is the glorious cloud of martyrs and witnesses, is yet loyal to the slayer of his countrymen, and ready to kiss his red, dripping hand. I am no more an Irishman than John Bright, but I refuse to desecrate language by giving such a vile thing a human name."

So much for the latest example of the Castle Bishop. Unhappily I am compelled to go back on a former one, but certain later proceedings of the Bishop of Elphin demand the reference. By every means in his power he has crossed the Irish movement, and in season and out of season, in ways which may be excused and which may not, endeavoured to bring it to failure. He publicly subscribes to the defence of the plan of campaign, while he warns his priests that if they aid it even privately he will inflict on them the severest punishment. He professes to go with the people, but he will allow no priest of his to take public action in their defence ; not even to the extent of presiding or speaking at a public meeting. He says he sympathises with them, but his actions go to show that he is more concerned for the collection of Lord de Freyne's rents than for their interests, their sufferings, or even their lives. One would imagine that the flagrant mistake of backing a man, whom a Dublin paper lately called "a drunken and obscene bully," for the representation of his county, would teach prudence for evermore ; yet we see him quite recently running successfully, for an office of trust, an Orange Freemason against one of his own subjects, whom he had complimented for his public-spirited and courageous conduct ! Dr. Gillooly is consistent only in being inconsistent. It is impossible for him to go right in anything touching public affairs. It seems natural in him to go wrong in everything not immediately concerned with his spiritual duties : and to enable him to compel his priests to follow his thrice unhappy example he has made void in their regard the constitution of the Church herself. He effectually provides that they shall not stand between their people and the oppressor by refusing collation to benefices, and making them curates or administrators—tenants at will—that is to say, serfs of an imperious despotism. He lives in a palace in Sligo, built with, I presume, the offerings of his flock. I do not reclaim against this ; on the contrary, I would surround every ecclesiastic with all the state and dignity becoming his sacred office; but in his magnificent surroundings he should not appear insensible to the wants of his people. There are tens of thousands of Dr. Gillooly's flock living in the bogs and mountains of Sligo and Roscommon under conditions dangerous to health and morals, and disgraceful to civilisation. For them he has no word of sympathy or defence ; for the rack-renters and exterminators, or the Government their accomplice, he has no sentence of condemnation or reproach.

Other examples equally flagrant of the Castle Bishop might be adduced if occasion required and space permitted. For the present let him be, remarking again that he has mistaken his day. The conditions of life in Ireland have hitherto secured him immunity. When the Irish people have secured the right to live they will turn their attention on him, and by means thoroughly effective and thoroughly Catholic they will procure that justice be done. We are taught that our Divine Lord would have died for the least soul on whom His image was stamped ; and His Vicar, whose glory it is to be instinct with His Spirit while invested with His power, has more regard for the salvation of that soul than for the feelings and positions of a thousand ecclesiastics who have brought their great office to naught. The Castle Bishop, in allying with the enemies of his people and of God, has forfeited the confidence of his subjects, and violated one of the first duties of his office. The blame will be ours if his ruinous and shameful policy be not made known to our Common Father, and the occasion made for ending him for ever. Our present position is one of mortal conflict with all the powers of evil. The Catholic ecclesiastic who stands against us, who stabs us in the back, who opens the citadel to the enemy, may be no worse in motive and intention than a misguided friend ; but we have to deal not with motives, but results—not with intentions, but with actions ; and if these be evil, if those be the acts of a traitor, he must, by the very necessity of the situation, be made to suffer the fate he has provoked.

I say, again, an anti-Scotch or anti-English bishop in either of the sister countries is impossible. If by accident he got appointed, his reign would be short. An anti-national French or Spanish, German or Italian bishop is not conceivable. Shall such a one be tolerated in Ireland alone, where the union of patriotism with religion is essential to the salvation of the people?

CONTENTS.

APPENDIX.

LETTERS.

THE ROMAN CIRCULAR.

SIR,—It is little thought of in this generation how much of the present energetic and hopeful condition of the Irish cause is due to the *Nation*. Thirty years ago, when Smith O'Brien and Mitchell were in banishment, Gavan Duffy in voluntary exile, the other trusted leaders of the people dead or scattered, A. M. Sullivan, with a courage and constancy never surpassed, undertook, almost alone, the hopeless and abandoned cause of Catholic Ireland, and sustained it with such versatility and power as to inspire fresh hope into hearts given up to despair, and to lay the foundations for the wonderful success our own day has witnessed.

But it may be doubted if, by any of the *Nations* of the past thirty years, any such service has been done as by that of last Saturday. In a situation unexampled, in a crisis of gravest danger, you have struck a note which will resound through the world, wherever men of the Irish race are found. On reading this paper my first feeling was one of profound gratitude to the good providence of God, which, I truly believe, inspired the words you have written ; and next, sir, I felt deeply grateful to you for so courageously and efficiently obeying the inspiration.

A frightful mistake has been made. Propaganda has changed sides and gone over to our enemies. We do not know by what pressure of influence, by what enormous and persistent slander, such a portentous perversion has been wrought. Our course is clear. It is carefully to consider our duty and do it, and with equal care to examine what are our rights, and maintain them. We will have against us prescription and the utmost dialectic skill ; but we have on our side the common inheritance of Catholic truth, and reason and justice added. By the aid of these I propose, sir, to examine the situation in the following letters ; and, as the questions involved are of the highest importance, I will take more time for them than is presently at my command. For the present I repel and reject the Circular of Propaganda—respectfully, considering the august body from which it comes ; firmly and energetically, as being opposed to facts as well as to my reason and conscience, and, in my opinion, calculated to ruin the best interests of Ireland and the Church. To apply a sentence of a great lawyer, "It has come forth without authority, and will go back without effect." As a practical mode of proving my sincerity, I repeat a subscription already paid, a course which is being followed by numbers. Meanwhile I remain, sir, yours,   AN IRISH CATHOLIC LAYMAN.

P.S.—It may be useful to inquire here, what has become of the first portion of this Circular. I am told by Latinists of skill that it could not have been commenced as it is given to us. Did it begin with a denunciation of the Land League, or what?—I. C. L.

THE ROMAN LETTER.

SIR,—In the letter to which you gave the unlooked-for honour of a place in your leading columns, I proposed to examine the nature and scope of the Papal authority, and, in the light of this inquiry, the value of the document presented for our acceptance by Propaganda.

No man can so well defend his own rights as he who is ready to yield prompt and full obedience to lawful authority. I declare myself, then, an Ultramontane of extremest type—if "extreme" can be correctly predicated of anything relating to the absolute. To the Holy Father I willingly grant all the power he claims, and this not more as a matter of faith than a conclusion of reason. For to him was given the command to "go and teach all nations," the power of Christ Himself to enforce and defend that teaching, and the inerrancy of which the Holy Spirit is the source and guard. Now, our Lord did not come on earth to form a school of philosophy or a sect among sects, but a spiritual kingdom, of which He is the real though unseen Sovereign.

The Church, in claiming such rights and franchises as are necessary for her action in the world, has not only the support of eighteen centuries of beneficence, but the right and authority of Christ dwelling within her, and whose practical providence she is.

, In constitution and essence the Church is a Divine and perfect society, sole remaining example in the world of the perfection with which its Creator originally endowed it. By this society God reveals Himself and his law to men; and of this revelation she is the depositary, guardian, and expounder. Her infallibility is a necessary corollary of these offices, since it would be contrary to the wisdom of God to reveal Himself for man's salvation without providing a means by which that knowledge could be certainly gained, and contrary to His justice to impose a law binding under the weightiest sanction without making that law patent to all who desired to live by it.

Of this perfect and Divine society the Pope is chief : not merely her executive, but in a special manner her head. For Christ being one

Person, his Vicar must also be one. He must be entitled to present himself to the world as inheriting the princedom of Peter. Assembling the councils of the Church, he dictates the matters of discussion, closes the debates, and gives authority and force to their decrees. All this goes to show that the plenitude of apostolic power is in the Papacy, and demonstrates, as De Maistre long ago pointed out, that it would be utterly irrational and preposterous to predicate a fallible head of an infallible body.

Not only do I gladly and thankfully embrace the doctrine of Papal infallibility in respect of the *matter* defined, but I assert for the Pope the right of declaring the range of subjects within the scope of definition. That is to say, the Pope, in imposing on us the duty of implicit obedience, is prevented by the Holy Spirit from transcending his own powers. He cannot declare as necessary to be believed any matter not contained in the deposit of the Faith. Non-Catholics commonly misapprehend the mental attitude of those within the fold to the Pope in the exercise of his chief office. For any such who may read those lines it may be useful to say that the revelation of God, as taught by the Church, is not a burden to be carried or a yoke endured with pain, but a priceless gift, a perennial source of intellectual delectation and spiritual joy—the one possession which never palls nor wearies, without which the world would be a howling wilderness, and life "not worth living." When this possession of inestimable value is increased by the Pope, rendering any truth from the abstract of the original but undefined deposit to the concrete of defined and certain dogma, the true faithful, so far from feeling any increase of the burden, are animated by a feeling of deepest gratitude. Surely no act of the late Pope's reign, long and glorious as it was, caused more universal joy than the definition of the Immaculate Conception. This, it may be observed, was an exercise of Papal authority which decided the question of infallibity long before it was voted by the Vatican Council. Such acts of the Pope are tests by which the spirit of Catholic obedience or its contrary are manifested. After this great act, and, still more, after the promulgation of the Papal nfallibility, many in Germany and some in England left the Church, showing that they were Catholics only in name, or held Catholic principles after a Protestant fashion. Like the Jews of old, who found our Lord's teaching hard, "they walked no more with him"—not that there was anything contrary to reason in the accents of Divine Wisdom, but that they themselves, hard-hearted and stiff-necked, would not bow to the humility of the Gospel.

But this perfect and grateful obedience is rendered to the Pontiff in the spiritual order only. In this he, like his Master, has the word of

Eternal Life, and to whom should we go but to him ? As Doctor of the Universal Church and Vicar of Christ, we listen with profound veneration, and accept *ex animo* all he teaches. But just in proportion to our prompt docility, when he has right to command, we claim the fuller liberty without the boundary of that right. The Pope has many characters and offices besides that which places him alone on earth. He is the Sovereign of the States of the Church ; he is private Doctor ; he is Ordinary of the diocese of Rome ; he is Patriarch of the West ; and in any of these capacities he is no more infallible than he is impeccable. Again, in the exercise of his office of teacher he speaks in many ways and with many degrees of authority—to individual prelates in private audience, in consistory by allocution, to provinces and peoples by brief and rescript, to the Universal Church by Bull. The style of each of these utterances is distinct, and the weight to be attached to them varied. All, indeed, are to be received with deepest respect ; but to one alone is to be given the homage of entire and implicit obedience. Finally, this absolute and unconditional authority is confined to the definition of matters of faith and morals alone, and to such matters of order and discipline as necessarily issue from them.

Besides the matters of moment in which the Pope personally intervenes, a vast amount of business is transacted by the various Congregations and by Propaganda ; and this naturally brings us to the present circular, which, I am deeply thankful to say, does not seem to be, in any true sense, a Papal utterance at all. Probably the Pope knew of some disciplinary circular being in preparation ; more probably he was not aware of its terms ; and most certainly he was not cognisant of its true nature. It is clear that a vast mass of business must pass through the courts which cannot possibly come under the personal observation of his Holiness. And we will best consult for his dignity by assuming that this document, as it has reached us, was never seen by him. Surely never before did anything so injurious and unfounded issue from the Roman Chancery. The style, so rash and violent, is unwholly unlike that of a Roman circular, and is much more nearly allied to what we are used to from the London *Times* or from Dublin Castle. Putting aside "Mr. Parnell and his objects" (as if these did not include the cause of Ireland and all that that implies), we are told that "some of his followers adopted a line of conduct different from instructions sent to the Irish bishops." We would like to know, first, in what sense the persons alluded to were "Mr. Parnell's followers," and what was "the line of conduct" they adopted. In a document of this gravity we want not ' vague assertions nor railing accusations, but the *ipsissima verba* of the peccant matter condemned. Further, we would like to be informed how instructions to the Irish bishops for their own guidance could be held to bind Mr. Parnell and his followers, to whom these instructions were not conveyed ; and why he or they were to be stigmatised and punished for not obeying instructions they never saw, and which were not meant for them.

It is difficult to analyse fully this extraordinary paper and preserve the respect due to Propaganda. Even now it is hard to believe it ever came from Rome. The most offensive and injurious thing about it is the implication underlying it all, that "Mr. Parnell and his followers" (the nine bishops and hundreds of priests who go to make up his committee included) are answerable for the crimes which are the natural and almost necessary outcome of English rule in Ireland ! And then what are we to think of the insults "offered to distinguished persons?" Is it wrong to believe that Forster, when he ravaged Ireland, filling the gaols with men a thousand times better than himself, was possessed by not one but many of the evil spirits who have their home in Dublin Castle ?

In respect of the judicial character of Propaganda, this document commits the unpardonable fault of deciding a cause not properly before it, in the absence of one of the parties and on *ex parte* evidence.

It is too much. In the language of the circular, "it is not to be tolerated" that the bitterest enemies of the Irish people and the Church of God shall with impunity poison the mind of the Sacred College, or that a recreant politician,* who is utterly discredited even with his own constituency, shall prevail against the eminent dignity, the splendid abilities, and priceless services of the Archbishop of Cashel.

With your permission, sir, in another letter I shall proceed to examine the causes which have led up to so dangerous a crisis in Irish politico-ecclesiastical affairs, and remain,

An Irish Catholic Layman.

THE ROMAN LETTER.

Sir,—Before entering on the grave and delicate question of the relations of the Irish Church with the various movements of the Irish people for the past half-century, it may be useful to enlarge somewhat on the circular ; and, in particular, on the use being made of it by our adversaries. By one mark this thrice unhappy document is judged and characterised, and that is the universal chorus of approval with which it has been received by the mortal enemies of the Papacy and of Ireland.

---

* Sir George Errington.

It may be that jibes and flouts and sneers have mingled with their approbation, but it is manifest all the same. Now, we know that "the children of this world are wiser in their generation than the children of light." Their instinct as to what makes for their cause is unerring; and we may hold it to be impossible that that which elicits unanimous approval from the impure and Godless press of England—true incarnation of all that is signified by "the world, the flesh, and the devil"—should further the interests of the Irish people or the Church of God. Leaving this argument, which will be found difficult to answer, let us observe more in detail the dangerous uses to which, as you point out so forcibly, the circular is being turned. A rev. canon of Achonry, in a letter to the *Freeman*, which, though short, is a model of illogical confusion, declares, by implication, the "Pope's Circular" to be binding, that he (the Holy Father) is above "criticism," and that we are to "obey God rather than man!" What is true in this letter is not new, and what is new we are happily not bound to accept as true. He ventures to speak for "all" his brethren in the ministry. I dare to say, from personal knowledge, that a majority of these, if they spoke at all, would give a very different account of their opinions.

Then Dean O'Brien "learns with dismay" that his people are about to do what they have a perfect right to do (is not this intimidation under the statute?), and tells them that such a course is "infidel," and that it must end "in the perpetual enslavement of your country;" moreover, that they are not to say or do anything in relation to the circular until their bishop has spoken. There is here, on one side or the other, a misdirection of the gravest kind. The organs of Propaganda tell us the circular is a purely ecclesiastical document, addressed to the bishops for their guidance and that of the clergy, and that it has no political or secular significance whatever. The dean, on the contrary, declares it to be urgently political and practical, so much so that the people are bound by it before it ever reaches them, or indeed himself, in authentic and authoritative form. What class of teaching does this belong to? The dean is fond of declaring himself "the Church." So we may grant him to be when he teaches his people true Catholic doctrine. So he surely is not when attempting by his spiritual power to destroy their lawful and salutary freedom. This, too, in presence of the fact that his venerated bishop wrote one of the most powerful and effective letters given to the press in support of the present movement.

Then at the head of the English Catholic press comes the *Tablet*, declaring to us wretched Irish that "the Pope has spoken," and the cause is at an end. No, O false and sophistical *Tablet!* the Pope has not so spoken, nor spoken at all. Would it not be well, O *Tablet!* when proceeding to lecture the Irish people on their duty to the Holy Father, to remember that the progenitors of those whom you represent permitted the most beastly tyrant of all history to proclaim himself their spiritual chief, and to oust the jurisdiction of the Vicar of Christ? If this is too long to remember, the present position of the Catholic body in England, without a single representative in the public life of their country, should inspire some reserve and modesty in their organ when addressing those whose courage and sacrifices gained them Emancipation.

A holy priest, speaking to the writer a few days ago, said: "We are tied; now is your time. The Irish laity saved the faith of Ireland before; with the help of God they will do it again." And they will do it, God and St. Patrick helping. The expression is consonant with historical fact, and not so presumptuous as would at first seem. For while there is the infallibility of the Pope, and the infallibility of the *Ecclesia Docens*, there is also in the body, the multitude of the true faithful, a practical infallibility. Illumined by the True Light, "which enlighteneth every man who cometh into the world," grasping the verities of the faith with a certainty surpassing, if it were possible, that of their own existence, prizing them above fortune and life itself, they are jealous of their possession with a holy jealousy, and repel with alarm and indignation any attempt to connect them with the changing forms of error or bend them to the exigencies of human affairs. Let any ecclesiastic, as unhappily ecclesiastics have done in the past, speak heresy or quasi-heresy from a pulpit where the faith is living and practical, at once the Catholic instinct of his hearers is alarmed—without perhaps always knowing the reason why they detect the fallacy lurking in the strange word. Their ears, accustomed to the sound of truth, detect the ring of the base metal, and they hasten to their and his spiritual chief to save them from the snares of error.

It is a remarkable fact, sir, that no reply on any side has been made, or even attempted, to the powerful and conclusive arguments drawn out by you from the wonderfully close analogy of the Veto. We are treated to all sorts of cloudy, irrelevant advices and exhortations; not in any one case has there been an attempt, successful or otherwise, to deal with your argument. Perhaps our adversaries are wiser in letting it alone. They would have been wiser still if they had not obtained by guile and fraud the intervention of the Sacred College. For they have now shown their hand; they have discovered to the world to what depths of slander and infamy they are prepared to go to gain even a momentary triumph over the people and the cause they hate with a preternatural and diabolical hatred. It will be our blame if we do not take the opportunity of tearing from the West-British, Whig-Liberal, Cawtholic faction the last shred of hypocritical pretence and falsehood, and exhibiting it to the Holy See and the world as a thing made up of self-seeking and corruption.   In this way we may turn evil into good, and hail the circular, when all emotions of amazement and indignation are allayed, as the cause of a new . and most salutary departure in Irish politico-ecclesiastical affairs.

I have. sir, the strongest conviction that all, or nearly all, of our later troubles have arisen from the alliance of certain of our chief ecclesiastics with the Whig-Liberal faction.   To trace the rise and consequences of this treaty, and the causes which have led to its partial but, we may hope, short-lived triumph, will be the aim of my next letter.—I am, sir, yours,

AN IRISH CATHOLIC LAYMAN.

THE IRISH CHURCH AND IRISH POLITICS.

" The religion and nationality of Ireland are inseparable."—*Archbishop Croke*.
" They (the Irish) mingle religion with their patriotism, and patriotism with their religion."—*Cardinal Newman*.
" I have never, for myself or others, directly or indirectly, sought or accepted a favour from the English Government."—*Dr. McHale*.
" If ever the Irish people fall away from the Irish Church it will not be the fault of the people."—*Dr. McHale*.

SIR,—In the course of what must needs be a historical retrospect, it will be useful to keep the above weighty and pregnant quotations in mind, since they go to show that what follows is not mere opinion, but fact written on the very face of our annals.

It is impossible for an unskilled writer to approach such a subject as the relations of the Irish Church with Irish politics without a most depressing feeling of incompetence.   For though one may have a certainty that the clear statement of the Irish question must carry conviction to all unprejudiced minds, that statement, embracing centuries of struggle, so many principles, so many facts, requires mental power and literary skill of the first order to do it justice.   The matter is in the minds of thousands : the power to crystallise it in lucid sentences, in orderly and harmonious sequence, belongs only to masters of style.

Nevertheless, feeling that the moment is opportune, and that the examination had better be made imperfectly than not at all, I will now proceed to lay bare what I conceive to be the causes of the present condition of Ireland.   We must seek these in antiquity, for what is seen around us is not the product of dead facts past and gone, but is the outcome of living and energising principles, as active now as at any period of our chequered history.

For nigh eight centuries two national ideas—two opposing sets of feelings, interests, and idiosyncracies—have struggled for supremacy on Irish soil. These are represented on the one side by a Government powerful, unscrupulous, ruthless; on the other, by a nation weak, disorganised, enslaved—opposing to absolute power invincible patience, to the most hideous and shameful injustice an indomitable though passive resistance. The first Anglo-Norman landed at Waterford, a hypocrite, a slanderer, a thief, and an assassin, and in these four characters his descendants and representatives remain to this day. He was a hypocrite, because (with or without Papal authority, it matters not) he came on pretence of reforming the Irish Church, while he had enslaved and corrupted his own ; a slanderer, employing hireling pens to defame the people whose ruin he contemplated; opening the gates of that flood of venemous falsehood which still flows at high water mark, covering truth with a deposit which can only be penetrated with great labour by true judicial minds. Of all the things we have had to bear surely the cruellest is that "persecution of slander" begun by Gerald Barry, and continued to our own day, when it finds worthy organs in the Macaulays, the Froudes, and the reptile anti-Irish press of England and of our own capital.

Like his chief progenitor, the Northern pirate, this Anglo-Norman was a robber. He coveted the lands of the natives, and never forbore to seize them when he had the power. Three times generally, a hundred times in detail, under one pretence or another, the whole surface of the country has been confiscated ; and, in the last change of owners, the principle of absolute personal property in the soil was introduced, which enabled the alien, finally settled in possession, to confiscate perennially all the gains the labour of his serfs wrung from the land. So atrocious has been the conduct of the Irish landowner that his own Parliament has been compelled to declare him unworthy to exercise any longer the rights of proprietorship, and has reduced him to the condition of rent-charger or annuitant where he lately ruled with power as absolute as a Turkish pasha or an American slaveowner. Finally, the Anglo-Norman adventurer was a murderer, since the life of a native was in his eyes as that of a wild beast ; and he never shrank from taking it when it stood between him and the object of his greed or ambition. The old brutal way being rather opposed to the spirit of the present day, his representative does his extermination now by less violent but equally sure methods. The great famine killed off or expatriated its millions. The little famine of 1879-1883 has quietly "removed" more than ever will be known till the bar of Eternal Justice is reached, and is still, with its various aids, emigrating its thousands and tens of

c

thousands. And so the ancient race—which will not be West-Britonised nor Protestantised, nor corrupted—is being done to death by all the arts discoverable by malice, and with a skill gained by centuries of experience.

The English Government in Ireland has never gained the moral right to exist, since it never aimed, nor, to do it justice, pretended to aim, at the well-being of the people it ruled.* Said the *Times*, "The Irish are gone with a vengeance." The *Times* was wrong. Enough remain to gain all the rights of freemen and citizens. Says Lord Derby, "It would pay us to spend some millions in emigrating this people." This cold-blooded and wooden-headed aristocrat passes for a statesman in England. Yet it needs little capacity to see that every healthy worker expatriated (and this is the only class which is going) weakens the strength of the Empire, lessens its productive power, and tarnishes the glory of the Sovereign's reign. Again Mr. Trevelyan goes down to Donegal and sees with his own eyes the misery of thousands of the best people in Ireland. Does he authorise outdoor relief? Does he set going public works, of which half-a-dozen of a remunerative and reproductive kind are possible in the West? Oh, no ; this would be true statesmanship, to which the Government of this country never rose. His remedy for imminent famine was the emigrant ship, which was not there, and the workhouse, which would not contain a twentieth part of the starving people needing aid. What everyone who speaks or writes for Ireland would need to proclaim and urge without ceasing is the fact —patent by its own confession—that the English Government in Ireland is actively and intensely hostile to every Irish interest, and never loses an opportunity of adding insult to the injuries it inflicts. This spirit pervades every function of Government from the least to the greatest. The English people have absolute power in Ireland, and they use it in a way inspired by national prejudice, which is intensified by centuries of falsehood, by trade jealousy, and by heretical malice. In its ultimate effect English rule means the domination of a powerless, but conspicuously Catholic people, by the chief Protestant power in the world. Emancipation was not granted to any principle of justice, but was compelled by other well-known causes. The ascendancy, the exclusiveness of the governing class, nominally displaced and destroyed, only drew itself together in secret league, and finds its suitable expression in the Orange Freemason ring in Dublin Castle. Long before

---

* Only yesterday Lord Salisbury said, in relation to Ireland, "We don't give representative institutions to Hottentots. We intend to exterminate another million of Irish, to give them twenty years of coercion ; and by that time they will be glad to take any favours we choose to offer." The twenty years' coercion has since expanded to coercion for ever and ever.

"boycotting" was publicly known by that name the ascendancy class practised it with eminent success. An Irish Catholic of the best stamp —that is, a good man and a good citizen—has no more chance of obtaining employment or honour, power, or indeed justice at the hands of this ring than he would have in China. Some Irish Catholics indeed are admitted within its narrow circle; and it may hereafter be useful to inquire what is the purpose of their adoption, what kind of work they do, and what manner of men they become. But they do not leaven the governing class nor change its spirit. They are employed to do its work and to give a colouring of fairness to the most bitter, the most comprehensive, and the most relentless tyranny the world ever saw.

But the fulness of time came, and the Providence of God raised up a man who to the rare union of qualities which make a leader of men added that active, absorbing passion of patriotism which has led him to devote his life to the emancipation of Ireland. Nothing of its kind in the world's history is comparable in deep and abiding interest to the revolution now proceeding under our eyes; the culmination of a struggle of centuries issuing in the proximate triumph of justice and of right; the reconquest by its true owners of a land in which but three years ago they had no root—a conquest achieved by force of ideas against absolute power arbitrarily exercised; by the peaceful legal combination of the humblest classes, aided by indomitable patience and a self-sacrifice often reaching the heroic degree.

A radical change is taking place in our social conditions which can neither be evaded nor stopped. The alien landlord, deprived of the power to work his will, good or evil as it might be, is departing to return no more. His (late) serf is lifting up his head and acquiring the carriage of a free man. A true reformation is taking place, and whether the "new order" be more or less perfect depends on the action of the Catholic Church, and on that alone.

With the exultation which fills every true Irish heart at the resurgence of the national life one painful, anxious thought mingles. It regards the conduct of a certain portion of the hierarchy—the dangers to faith and morals to which their action gives rise, and its probable effect in retarding or disfiguring the social edifice now in process of reconstruction. The treatment of this part of my subject I will ask your leave to reserve for another letter.

Yours, &c.;

AN IRISH CATHOLIC LAYMAN.

THE IRISH CHURCH AND IRISH POLITICS.

Sir,—When O'Connell wrung from an unwilling Legislature the Act
which made him one of the most beneficent as he was himself one of the
greatest of men, he emancipated a people who were in many ways as
unfit for as they were unused to freedom. Their slavish submission to
their former masters was continued long after it ceased to be imperative.
The habit of association for the conduct of affairs, the noble and disinterested public spirit developed in free communities, were almost wholly
wanting. The various orders of the social hierarchy had either no
cohesion or were at deadly enmity with each other. Emancipation itself
was mainly theoretical. It gave the Irish a nominal freedom—permission
to follow their own destiny on their own soil, the governing classes taking
care to retain the shaping of that destiny and the ownership of that soil.
"Catholics," said Sir Robert Peel to the old Tory who reproached him
with raising Papists to the magistracy, "will be eligible, but they won't
be appointed;" and they are not appointed to this day, save on condition of attorning to the English interest and doing their master's work.

Two classes there were who were capable of completing the social,
industrial, and political emancipation of Ireland, the Catholic aristocracy
and the Catholic Church. The people were always ready. The strength
and courage, the virtue and self-sacrifice of the Irish race are in the
masses, and they grow stronger as the lowest stratum (in rank) is
approached. There is no possible height of patriotism, of religion, of
devotion to every great and noble end, to which they are not willing and
ready to be led, if leading there be but unhappily "light and leading"
have long been wanting in the quarters from which they might have been
expected.

Taking first the Catholic aristocracy, the natural leaders of the
people in the public order, it may well be doubted if the world's history
shows anything more thoroughly contemptible than the character and
conduct of this class. Instead of using their newly-found liberty to
raise their fellow-Catholics from poverty and ignorance, they rushed to
seize the fruits of a victory in the gaining of which they had no part.
O'Connell's action was paralysed and thwarted by the selfishness and
corruption of his surroundings. The nobles voted him "vulgar" and
"violent." They went with their class and order, and so far from con-
cerning themselves with the welfare of the people, they would not
acknowledge the man who gave them the freedom of which they were
unworthy. The Catholic landowners were so much engaged in following,
and often surpassing the rack-renting and evicting practices of their
Protestant fellows that they had neither time nor inclination to attempt
the foundation of a better order of things. And so the unhappy country

struggled on from famine to famine, from convulsion to convulsion, till Davitt and Parnell and the Land League came to raise it to renewed hope and a higher aim and life. This contemptible and emasculate Catholic landocracy had their opportunity. They might have led the people in the paths of justice and right, of peace and progress : they preferred to go over to the enemy ; they also preferred to stand by their class and order, though the majority of these were descendants of Cromwell's troopers, who despised them while they accepted their aid to trample on the people. Their profound selfishness and meanness, their want of self-respect and Catholic spirit, were in nothing so well seen as in their joining in numbers the Orange Emergency Eviction Committee, which had for its avowed object the extermination of Catholics and the replanting of the country with "loyal" Protestants ! *One of the very few personally respectable men among them chose the height of Forster's muck-running to get sworn in of the Privy Council and to join the Kildare Street Club. †Another has joined worthy companions in producing an elaborate scheme for the further development of emigration. Hardly one can be named who gave evidence of any desire to do his duty to Ireland. The great famine ended a multitude of Catholic "shoneens," ignorant and insolent, corrupt and corrupting, swearing, drinking, fox-hunting boors, a curse to the country and a disgrace to the Church within whose borders they barely came. The land courts and the land movement may be trusted to end the remainder.

There remained that great institution, the Church of God, set by Divine Wisdom to repair the defects of human society and restore it, as far as the loss of man's integrity permits, to its original condition. The spirit of the Catholic Church, however it may be occasionally deflected by human weakness, is the spirit of justice. It emancipated the slave, and made the poor in all times and countries the object of its tenderest concern. It stood for legitimate freedom against German emperor and Tudor king, defending human liberty as the surest foundation of religion. The history of the Middle Ages, from the eighth to the fourteenth century, is mainly composed of the struggles of the Popes to preserve it from the attacks of tyrants. In various times and places it is true that ecclesiastics have been found on the wrong side, but this was when the State had intruded its baneful influence. The nomination to benefices on the part of the Sovereign led to the gradual decay of Catholic spirit among the clergy. The Church in France is now suffering martyrdom because a section of its members allied itself with a corrupt court and a worthless aristocracy ; and whenever she loses her influence and

---

* The O'Conor Don.
† Christopher Talbot Redington.

fails in her Divine work, it is because of this unnatural connection with her and our enemies. To her it might be held to fall, with special suitability, to reform and refound society in Ireland. For to her it is due that the Irish nation exists as it is, or exists at all in any condition above savage life. To the strict morality she imposes are due the wonderful vitality and recuperative power of the Irish race ; to her humanising influence the amenity and courtesy of manner which distinguish the Irish peasant above all his fellows. To the Church, which sustained him in a struggle of unrivalled intensity and duration, he might naturally have looked to complete his triumph ; and in happier circumstances he would not have looked in vain.

But while nation and Church emerged victorious from the conflict, they bore, and long must continue to bear, the scars and wounds of that mortal strife. It would be preposterous to expect the arts of peace to flourish in times of war. It would be still more absurd to expect that the Irish Church should display, when the time of combat was over, the beauteous developments which adorn her in times of peace—the flowers and fruit of the counsels of perfection which, where the fulness of her power prevails, make the earth itself a paradise and give her children a foretaste of heaven.

Frankly, the Church was unequal to the task before her when Emancipation struck the fetters from her limbs. A later "discipline of the secret" had tied, as it still ties, her tongue. Though she has at her command the pulpit, the press, and the platform, though of a race one of whose gifts is oratory, she is rarely heard, and her eminent speakers may be numbered by units instead of hundreds. This is one of the results of the repression of her natural life and the paralysis which falls on the noblest faculties when unused.

Those who form their opinion of the Church's power from her action in this country, thwarted on all sides and depressed as she has been, have little notion of the effect she produces when her Divine powers have free play.* The least acquaintance with the centuries succeeding the fall of the Roman Empire suffices to show that she everywhere displayed an amazing vigour and resource in laying the foundations of the Christian

---

* Such astonishing progress has been made since this was written that it is now a simple matter of duty to point to the short career of the present Archbishop of Dublin as an example of the beneficence of the Church's action. In a few years he has done a life's work. The poor, the sick, the erring, the orphan—every phase of human want and suffering—are by him sought out and relieved. No week passes in which he does not lay a foundation stone or open some house of religion or charity— no day that he does not visit, encourage, and reorganise some one of the numbers of beneficent institutions in our midst. Nor do his proper labours, multiplied as they are, prevent him from striking many a stout blow for justice and truth, and showing in defence of his people a courage, versatility, and power as rare in the metropolitan see as they are beyond any praise of mine.

order of society, from whence has come to us everything of value in modern civilisation. The action of the secular power in the social and moral orders was little more than a disturbance or perversion of the beneficent work of the Church. In the religious orders, pre-eminently in the Benedictine, were contained the most fruitful and active principles of true civilisation; while their government gave the best example of the union of freedom with authority. To impute to the Church then the power to reform society and place it on a sound and progressive basis is simply to declare what she has done before, and may at any time do again. Her canon law embraces the principles of natural equity and the higher law revealed by the Gospel; and on these must all just secular legislation proceed.

We are contemplating what the Irish Hierarchy might have done. What it did do was unhappily very different. And this makes it necessary in the present exigency, to declare that, while the Irish Church has succeeded magnificently in the spiritual order, she has failed signally, if not utterly, in the temporal. Not without a grave sense of responsibility is this charge made; and some distinctions and reservations should properly precede it. When using the word Hierarchy then, I do so only collectively, and as regards the Church's corporate action. The Providence of God has always provided that the Hierarchy in this country should include prelates as truly and ardently Irish, as they are Catholic. It is clear that, whatever may be said of the failure of the Church to use its enormous power for the public good, no blame can attach to the bishops who would have done their duty if permitted. Neither do I presume to impute to the policy followed by any bishop the slightest shade of moral wrong. Such an imputation would be as abhorrent to my sense of duty and of fitness, as it is wholly unnecessary for the effect of the argument. It is no just reproach to a good and zealous bishop that he is not also a wise politician or a sagacious statesman. It is my happiness and advantage to know some of the prelates whose public conduct will be most severely arraigned. They are one and all men of simple and most edifying lives, exemplary in the discharge of the essential duties of their great office, and of such personal holiness that we may well believe they would not shrink from the striking of

> ——"A deeper, darker dye,
> In purple of their dignity,"

did country or faith require the sacrifice of their lives. Again, in estimating the public action of our prelates, it cannot be overlooked that they have to view questions from all sides; that they are charged with the salvation of every baptised Christian within the bounds of their jurisdiction; and that prudence, one of the first of episcopal virtues, is

from its very nature exceedingly apt to degenerate into timidity, and
to ally itself with the selfishness from which the human heart is seldom
entirely free. In reviewing their political action, as I intend doing with
the utmost freedom consistent with due respect, I again declare that I
am Catholic before all and beyond all. As, with God's help, I am ready
to sacrifice everything, even life itself, rather than yield one jot or tittle
of the inestimable treasure of the faith—supposing that the indivisible
could be divided—so for Ireland I can desire no less than the good I
claim for myself, and would rather see her remain a martyr till the crack
of doom than she should lose the glorious distinction of being the most
Catholic of nations.

But martyrdom is not the normal condition of a nation's life; nor is
it desirable save when inevitable.

Ireland has had a long spell of it, and her children may now
hope that in the councils of Divine Wisdom a brighter and happier
day is approaching. It is to hasten that day that I dare point out the
gravest obstacles to its advent, and to declare that these exist not in the
machinations of our enemies so much as in the errors of our friends. "A
man's enemies shall be those of his own household;" and in the anti-
Irish part taken by some of our prelates, in the dry rot of Whiggery of
the Irish Church, lie the chiefest obstacles to our onward course. Now,
I do not mean to charge any Irish bishop with being a Whig. That
would be, in my view, a scandalous libel, as I believe Dr. Johnson was
right in declaring that a certain nameless personage was the first of the
race. But that the action of many has been and is pro-Whig unhappily
needs no proof. As this letter has already reached its proper limit, the
opening of what has always seemed to me the most melancholy and
dangerous chapter in recent Irish history must be reserved till next.

I am, sir, yours, &c.,

AN IRISH CATHOLIC LAYMAN.

_____

THE IRISH CHURCH AND IRISH POLITICS.

SIR,—It is surely an evil day for Ireland when it has become necessary to arraign at the bar of public opinion the action of a considerable
portion of her hierarchy. The creation of this necessity is not the work
of the Irish people, but of their enemies; and on them be the blame,
if such there be. Assuming it to exist, as we are amply justified in
doing, the gravity of the facts, and the importance of the principles
involved, require that the indictment should be drawn with the utmost
frankness. In the crisis which exists at this moment in Irish affairs,
polite euphemisms would be wholly out of place.

Again declaring that I do not presume to judge the moral nature of the action in question, I have nevertheless to charge that portion of the hierarchy which has made and makes common cause with the English Government in Ireland with the violation of several of the gravest obligations belonging to the episcopal office. Their action has been in many respects a practical abandonment of their duty as guardians of faith and morals. As publicists they have failed to vindicate the principles of the Christian order, as patriots they sided with the open and avowed enemies of their country.

Short of the charge of heresy no weightier could be brought. It is not done without reflection, nor without the sanction and approval of many whose characters, training, and sacred office satisfy the writer that the task he has undertaken is not only justifiable but meritorious. Individual examples and detailed proofs of the truth of the indictment will be forthcoming. Meanwhile, it will be useful to point out that as on Irish soil two hostile and mutually destructive principles have combated for centuries, so within the circle of the Irish hierarchy the two have always found advocates and defenders. In old times we have had bishops of the Pale ; now we have bishops of the Castle ; formerly the statute of Kilkenny, now the "suppression " in many dioceses of any priest brave enough to show any feeling of patriotism. It is clear that if the policy with which the late Dr. McHale was identified represented every Irish and Catholic interest, that identified with the late Cardinal Cullen was subversive and destructive of all embraced by these words. If Dr. McHale truly represented, as we know he did, the Irish people and the Church of God, the Cardinal on every point where the two prelates were in opposition represented the enemies of both. No good end can be served by hiding or paltering with this clear issue—namely, that if in the present the Archbishop of Cashel and the Bishop of Meath be right in standing boldly in defence of the spiritual and temporal interests of the Irish race, the Cardinal McCabe and the present Archbishop of Tuam *must* be wholly and ruinously wrong.

"Pontius Pilate," wrote the Bishop of Orleans to Napoleon III., when charging him with betraying the Pope, "has been placed in the pillory of our creed, not for commanding, or even desiring, the commission of the greatest crime of all history, but for not preventing it when in his power." In like manner, by no straining of argument, but by direct consequence of his action or inaction, the Castle Bishop is in a great degree answerable for the suffering and crime, the untold misery and sin, arising from our condition for the past fifty years; for he it was who broke he unity of the Irish Church and paralysed its action—he it was who, abandoning the straight and noble paths of Irish nationality and Catholic principle, allied himself with the basest forms of heretical pravity, and imperilled the very faith of Ireland in return for places for corrupt Whig lawyers. When prompt and decided action was needed, he temporised ; when strict adherence to principle was necessary, he compromised; and in these two words, "temporise" and "compromise," are found the unhappy source of all our more recent sufferings. The proof unhappily is on the face of our history. At one of the first meetings of the hierarchy after emancipation, Dr. McHale proposed, as the Church's first duty in the public order, to formulate, with aid of jurist and canonist, the claim of the Irish people. 1st, to the most elementary of all rights, the right of existence by their labour on the soil of their country. 2nd, to the just and impartial administration of the law—such as it was ; and 3rd, the right of the Irish Catholic people to Irish and Catholic education. He was withstood in this as in many another proposal, the carrying of which would have begun, if not wrought out, our real emancipation. His sagacity, courage, and patriotism was brought to nought by the inconsistent, the timid, and time serving. Some provision for Irish Catholic education was the necessary complement of emancipation. Some consistency, courage, and adherence to principle were all that were wanting to provide that the Irish Catholic people should have Irish Catholic schools. The hierarchy were wanting in all three, and, with a blindness which amazes us yet, consented to a compromise condemned by Catholic principles, and issuing in a system neither Irish nor Catholic—save by accident. From this compromise have issued, in congruous and monstrous series, the Model Schools, the Godless Colleges, and the Queen's (and now the Royal) University. From this has also arisen the destruction of thousands of young men whom a Catholic education would have saved, and the absence of a truly educated class of Irish gentry, who would have long ere this led the country to freedom and peace. John of Tuam, indeed, strove like a hero, as he was, for freedom and purity in education ; but he strove almost alone, and the most powerful external agency of the Church—the Christian School— was given up to our enemies by the sworn defenders of the Christian order. When treating, as I hope to do separately, the subject of education, some hints will be given of the later conduct of this all-important matter. I now declare the first fatal compromise by Dr. Murray to be the most unjustifiable and ruinous violation of parental and national right ever perpetrated by a Catholic prelate or accepted by a national hierarchy. Suffice it now to say, that on a subject peculiarly its own the Irish Church utterly broke down, and, as a last and worst result, we have now the scandalous compromise of the "Royal" University—the same university, be it noted, which spends twice as much on the entertainment of its senate as it does on the encouragement of the unfortunate students confided to its care.

If I were writing a history of Ireland, many chapters could be given to the action of ecclesiastics from 1830 to 1850. As it is, I can only point out that our Churchmen were incapable, or at all events did not attempt, to undertake the work of which the Catholic aristocracy was not worthy. The first necessity after political emancipation was industrial. The first duty was to bring the law of the land into conformity with justice and the law of God. Three-fourths of the people of Ireland dwelt on its soil strangers in their own country, subject to be deprived of land and life at the will of an alien and too often hostile proprietary. That they were so deprived in hundreds of thousands, we know too well. To this evil condition may be traced two of the principal defects in the national character. The serf deceives his master to escape the lash, and drinks to drown the feeling of degradation. Our later history, that of a people declining in numbers and wealth, acquiring little by little, by force of *quasi* insurrection, the commonest rights of citizens, is proof of the absurdity of endeavouring to found a new order on such conditions as were present in Ireland fifty years ago. Now, all the bishops had mastered the tract "of justice." They knew the labourer was worthy of his hire; they knew that what a man made was justly his; and they looked on and saw their people rack-rented and evicted, scourged and decimated, and they made no combined or effective effort for their protection.

Had the Irish Church formulated the Irish claim fifty-four years ago— had it done this most urgent and necessary duty any time since, it would have discharged some part of its responsibility; for the demonstration of the justice of the claim would have gone far to make its realisation actual. Every man, patriot or self-seeker, true or false, who entered public life would have it as a standard by which his conduct was to be directed and judged. And the interposing of the sanction of the Irish Church to a State paper, demonstrably true in its propositions, and indefeasible in its conclusions, would have silenced then as now the monstrous falsehoods and calumny with which we are assailed.

In the organisation of the Church of Ireland exists a power never yet used for Ireland. It is a power co-extensive with the island, touching and controlling all within it, Catholic and non-Catholic. Did the Irish bishops unite at any time on the attainment of any Irish or Catholic measure, their organisation would make them irresistible. The land question could have been settled half a century ago, and the strife of classes prevented by the stoppage of landgrabbing, the erection in every parish of a tenants' defence association, with the parish priest for president, and the assertion of the principle, now happily in force, that no man should take a farm evicted for non-payment of an unjust rent. This would have been a land law making the inequitable and, as events have too well proved, inefficient operation of the present Land Courts unnecessary. The first duty incumbent on the leaders of the Irish people, either in the lay or ecclesiastical orders, was the protection by law of their lives and properties. Neither one nor other was equal to the task. Once, indeed, in the pastoral of the Synod of Thurles, a note was struck which looked like the awakening of the Church to a sense of the duty before it. Like every pronouncement of the kind—whether as regards the right of the Irish people to regulate their own affairs according to the spirit of the constitution, the land question, or education—it was a theory only, never rendered into fact. Since then, many times over, the hierarchy has assembled, and with like result. It never meets now without inspiring a feeling of pain and fear—of pain that another opportunity be added to the many already wasted; of fear lest some mistake more egregious than the last be added to a list already too long. Our bishops meet and discuss, resolve and memorialise with something worse than nothing for result—namely, the general conviction that their fatal want of unity is prolonging indefinitely the nation's decadence, and endangering its very existence. A real union on any of the questions now agitating the country would insure by the very fact the attainment of the end proposed. On the last occasion their lordships addressed the country they declared they would "lead" the people. We have not heard since in what direction. It may save some mistakes to declare now that if the people are to be led it will not be through the mire of Whiggery, nor into the shadow of Dublin Castle. In my next letter I propose to examine the effect of Cardinal Cullen's administration on Irish affairs, and then that of the prelates who have succeeded to his policy and traditions.

Yours,

AN, IRISH CATHOLIC LAYMAN.

THE REIGN OF CARDINAL CULLEN.

SIR,—The singularly able and thoughtful letter of "Lux Sit," in your last number, dealing with one of the most dangerous elements of the anti-Irish conspiracy, induces me to diverge for a moment from the principal subject of this letter to press a portion of his argument into service here.

The Irish question is eminently historical. It is also essentially Catholic. Therefore, the power which aims at the extermination or corruption of the Irish people, excludes history and religion from the National Schools. This is the position of "Lux Sit," and it is incontrovertible. It is evident he knows more about the subject than he cares to tell; and he apologises for a warmth of language which some may think unseemly. Now, will you permit me to suggest to him with the respect inspired by the excellent work he is doing, that the time has passed for reticence? When the faith and very existence of Ireland are threatened forbearance, no matter who is in question, where frankness is necessary, may well be deemed inexcusable timidity. When a man's life and honour are assailed, he is justified in taking the strongest measures in defence. We are at this moment threatened by an unnatural and monstrous combination. Our hereditary enemies and some of our spiritual chiefs have invaded the Vatican. They threaten us in the very centre of our spiritual life. The former have exhausted against us the whole catalogue of human crime, and in conjunction with the latter they have succeeded for the moment in imposing on some members of the Sacred College the belief that the Irish people are thieves and murderers.

Taking the single weapon of truth, our duty is to expose that unhappy delusion; to say to the Sacred College, or—if our adversaries will insist on the circular being his own act—to the Holy Father, with the utmost respect, but with unalterable firmness: "You have been shamefully deceived and betrayed by your enemies and ours. We are still the law-abiding, justice-loving Catholic and Irish people we have always been; and those who would make us answerable for the crimes bred of their own savage tyranny add slander of the basest sort to their other iniquities." I say, then, to "Lux Sit," go on and tell all that needs to be told of the sickening story of Irish Catholic education. Archbishop Murray justly bears the largest portion of the blame due for the wretched muddle into which this question of primary importance has fallen. A true bishop of the Pale, he thought the Irish race should be content with toleration, and grovel at the feet of their taskmasters. When an Irish prelate takes suit and service with Dublin Castle he does not always succeed in keeping his orthodoxy from suspicion. When Dr. Murray undertook the defence of the Queen's Colleges, and publicly rebuked Frederick Lucas for calling them "Godless," if he did not pass the line which separates Catholic principle from its opposite, he went perilously near doing so.

Not he, however, but one still more eminent, must bear the charge of causing the decadence into which a portion of the Church in Ireland has fallen in these later days. To many who only knew the late Cardinal in his office of Churchman it would look like "flat blasphemy" to say it. Yet those who are familiar with the history of the last thirty-five years will have no difficulty in assenting to this portentous conclusion, that since Oliver Cromwell landed on her shores no greater calamity befell Ireland than the advent of Cardinal Cullen.

The sword of the regicide endangered her physical life; the policy of the Cardinal, aptly called "stone blind," struck a deadlier blow at her faith, although nothing was farther from his Eminence's intention. Worse than the famine which sent its tens of thousands to Paradise by the road of patient suffering, his policy, by destroying the national organisation, and begetting Fenianism as clearly as any cause ever begot a consequence, has sent its thousands to the other place. It paralysed the national life of Ireland, and retarded her advancement for thirty years. Helping to fasten upon the country for a whole generation the deadly incubus of landlordism, it is, in part, answerable for the misery, ruin, and crime that iniquitous system brought forth. To use the words of Michael Davitt—words as true as they are forcible—the very damned cry out from the midst of their torments, invoking justice not only on their oppressors but on the policy which maintained the land laws for half a century longer than they would otherwise have existed.

At another time it may be desirable to inquire as to the special purposes of the Cardinal's mission and its general effect on Irish ecclesiastical affairs. For the present we must hasten on to the relation of the most lamentable chapter of Irish history since the Union. The famine was past. Though walking skeletons, emaciated creatures half alive, still horrified the stranger on the public ways, the wonderful recuperative powers of the race, their buoyant energies, were beginning to reassert themselves. Then it was that Frederick Lucas and Gavan Duffy,* and others as earnest, if less eminent, came together and vowed that landlordism should never in Ireland create another famine. They organised a formidable party—so formidable that it threatened the existence of the Government. They went on the lines of independent opposition, the very same as those which two years ago led Parnell to victory—the only one which can by any possibility lead to the achievement of any good for Ireland. Had the party of 1851 been as honest as that of 1881 all that has been gained in the latter year would have been gained in the former.

---

* Now Sir Charles Gavan Duffy.

But, unhappily, the Irish party had its dishonest and corrupt section. At the critical moment, when everything depended on the maintenance of its unity, the baser part opened secret negotiations with the enemy, and, despite of pledge and oath, openly and flagrantly sold themselves for place. The treachery might have been overcome ; the true men met the false on the hustings and through the country, and would have beaten them—oh, shame and horror to have it to say!—if the Cardinal had not interposed, and entered into secret alliance with the suicide-swindler Sadleir, and the perjured apostate Keogh. Dr. Brown, of Elphin, "gave poor Billy a chance ;" and though the Cardinal did not openly enter into the fray, his uncle, Father Maher, and others, directly inspired by him or under his authority, defended the traitors in the public press. The crosier of St. Laurence O'Toole fell with crushing weight on any priest who had the courage and principle to stand by the right. The cry of "No priests in politics" was raised—meaning none save those who undertook the defence of political corruption. It was a sad and sickening spectacle then, it is sad and sickening to-day ; for its consequences remain, and its example is being followed, in less flagrant fashion it may be, for public opinion is now more powerful, and political intelligence more widely diffused. We know what followed. Duffy abandoned the struggle, and found fame and fortune under the Southern Cross. More fortunate in many minds, Lucas gave his life for the cause, and died a true martyr, not so much of the Roman miasma as of a broken heart. It may well be doubted if the faith of any other people on the face of the earth would have borne without revolt the spectacle of a Cardinal leagued in politics with some of the most infamous characters in Irish history—men as void of religion as they were corrupt in politics. There is some compensation in the thought that this vile faction was struck, as if by a thunderbolt, in the very hour of its triumph. Its members, with one notable exception, became fugitives from justice, and Keogh alone remained to bite the hand that raised him, and pour out his venom on the Church and the people he disgraced.

Since the Union it is the saddest page of Irish history. One single consolation it has—it can never be repeated.

AN IRISH CATHOLIC LAYMAN.

CARDINAL CULLEN AND CARDINAL McCABE.

SIR,—In an unhappy hour for his own reputation, for Ireland, and the Church, Cardinal Cullen was drawn from his retirement in Rome to do here a work which was in itself one of capital importance, namely, to tighten the bonds of discipline, relaxed by centuries of warfare, and

repair breaches in the sacred walls made by many a desperate assault.
Admirably fitted for this work by great abilities and acquirements, by
strength of will and inflexible adherence to what he thought right, and
by the true ecclesiastical spirit, he failed because he was profoundly
ignorant of the people he had to govern and the enemies with whom he
had to contend. With the latter he entered into alliance ; from the
former his separation became wider and more hopeless to the end. . All
of Irish that remained of him was his name. Had he stayed in Armagh
he might have acquired some knowledge of Irish affairs. In Dublin the
Cawtholic Whigs surrounded and possessed him and used his vast
influence for their own ends, to his destruction as a patriot bishop.
Clothed as Papal delegate, with enormous powers, he ruled supreme in
ecclesiastical affairs, with the effect of deepening differences into irre-
concilable antagonisms, dividing still more definitely the Church into two
parties, and destroying her unity of action. Coming from a country honey-
combed by secret societies of the anti-social and anti-Christian type he
brought with him such a dread of societies of any kind that he would not
permit the introduction into the archdiocese of the most useful and
admirable Young Men's Society, founded by Dean O'Brien, although its
primary rule is monthly confession, and the spiritual director of each
branch has a veto on all its proceedings. Accustomed, in fine, to the
Italian character, he did not know, nor trust, the loyalty and constancy
of his own countrymen to every person or cause rightly claiming their
allegiance. The English Government exhausted the resources of
diplomacy in the Veto struggle. When it was over in external form it
continued in secret, the diplomatists on the English side being the Castle
bishops and the Catholic aristocracy. It continued with varying success
till Cardinal Cullen removed to Dublin, when the English won "all along
the line." They would have given millions for its concession ; they got
it for nothing. It is at this moment eating into the vitals of the Irish
Church and reducing her to impotence. In many dioceses the patriot
priest is a mark for episcopal disfavour. One would imagine from the
action of some bishops that it was their intention to let the Irish people
work out their deliverance by aid of any guidance but that of the Church.
With one or two conspicuous exceptions, all the appointments made by
the Cardinal during his long reign were either anti-Irish or non-Irish. It
is possible that many of the venerable personages included in either
category may repel the classification as unjust. Unhappily the facts
are against them. In a struggle like the present, for very life,
neutrality is opposition. "A priest without politics is a Whig in
disguise." As if made to confirm the argument, the Maynooth meeting
and the resolutions of last week appear. These exhibit the bishops

signing them in the position of persons who proclaim that they ardently desire certain things, while, though they have ample power, they do not take one step to attain them. To people at a distance the resolutions may look well. To people nearer home they seem only one other intimation to the Government that in pursuing their policy they have nothing to fear from the majority of the Hierarchy. They were made under a Veto no less real because not expressed in any former treaty, and they act according to their kind. Like the Bourbons, many bishops seem to learn and forget nothing. For them the wonderful conquest of the Irish party during the last three years are non-existent; to them the Monaghan election appeals in vain. They will go on resolving and memorialling till the battle is won, and they will then look on an Irish nation constituted without their aid, and in which their influence will hardly be felt. Is it too much to hope that even now, at the last moment, putting aside timid counsels, they will join frankly and thoroughly with their people in completing in its best and highest sense the victory already half gained ?

A French journalist, misinterpreting Mr. Parnell in one of his visits to Paris, made him declare that the Archbishopric of Dublin was in the nomination of the English Government. The meaning, of course, was clear : that the Metropolitan See was always filled by a West British—that is, anti-Irish—prelate. The fact, unfortunate enough at all times, became disastrous when in filling it Cardinal Cullen wielded, in addition to his own, the Papal authority. Trusted implicitly in Rome, intimately acquainted with the whole *entourage* of the Papal Court, himself one of the chief members of the Sacred College, no cause could succeed which he did not favour—none, however just, could prevail when he stood against it. To his representation of the Irish question the Errington Mission and the Circular are due; nor would the miserable race of English Catholic backbiters gain a hearing in Rome did not the great Cardinal's views give a colour to their slanders. Peace be to him ! In the midst of his disastrous mistakes the Irish people gave to his splendid abilities the homage of their respect; nor with so much to forgive him will they forget the noble appearance he made in the O'Keeffe trial, nor the calm dignity with which he rebuked the "ascendency" spirit of Chief Justice Whiteside.

For many a day the influence of Cardinal Cullen will be felt in the Church in Ireland. We see its effect day after day in the enforced absence from the popular ranks of the best of the priesthood, and the growing power of the pro-Whig faction. From the bishops he appointed it has gone to the second order of the clergy, and we can only look to

D

time and to the wisdom inspired by the Holy Spirit to eradicate it.   For the present we have to leave him, to examine the policy of his eminent successor.

For this there is not the palliation of long residence abroad. Living all his life in Ireland, Cardinal McCabe has bettered the example of Cardinal Cullen in its most anti-Irish features.   Under his administration the See of Dublin has got further estranged from the Irish cause, and the chain of Castle servitude more firmly bound on priests and people.   The Cardinal seems to have lost all idea of Irish feeling, and to have got quite across with the current of public opinion. The spirit now prevailing has had some astonishing manifestations.   In 1875, Ireland celebrated the centenary of her greatest son.   To the public rejoicing religion added the dignity of her holiest services; and the Archbishop of Cashel spoke the panegyric of the Liberator, with Cardinals Franchi and Cullen amongst his auditors.   Seven years later, Ireland celebrated the unveiling of his statue.   Alas ! no religious ceremonial added its ineffable charm to the public rejoicing.   Daniel O'Connell might have been a Turk, Jew, or Pagan for all the Church in Ireland did on that day in honour of his remembrance.   Again, in the most creditable effort Ireland made to revive her crushed industries, the Church in Dublin lent no aid ; and the reason given for its being withheld was at least as extraordinary as the withholding.

But these are trivial matters in comparison with what follows. Four years ago Ireland was threatened with one of her periodical law-made famines.   Government got full warning of the impending calamity.   As usual, inspectors were sent who saw what their masters wanted them to see, and no more.   The peril became imminent. Davitt inaugurated the Land League, and Parnell crossed the Atlantic in mid-winter to seek aid for the starving people of Mayo and Donegal. What did Cardinal M'Cabe in the emergency ?   He assures us he felt for the people !   I am not concerned to deny the sympathy, but was it not like the faith from which no works follow ?   What he *did* in the course of the struggle with famine and evil laws was to issue two pastorals condemning the action taken on the popular side.   These, no doubt, contained excellent Catholic doctrine, but had they had the royal arms at the top, and been dated from Dublin Castle, they could not have been in effect more truly Government proclamations.

Wherever, the world over, English influence penetrates, the man of Irish name and faith is confronted by that "persecution of slander" which has ever been one of England's most potent weapons.   In one of his journeys to Paris, Mr. Parnell met the leading French journalists, and put before them the truth of the Irish question.   Amongst others,

Rochefort came, and forthwith Mr. Parnell was accused of seeking to ally the Irish cause with the Red Republic. Again the accusation was repeated, although it had been shown that Rochefort came as the editor of the *Express* might come with the editor of the *Freeman* to wait on a distinguished foreign statesman. How true it is that one man may steal the horse, while another may not look over the hedge, although he may have no intention to steal. Were there no other alliances in which the honour of Ireland was besmirched and Catholic interests sacrificed? We shall see.

The late Pope, of happy and glorious memory, had in Europe three deadly enemies—Count Cavour, Napoleon III., and Lord Palmerston. Against Catholic principles and legitimacy everywhere, the chief aim of this confederacy of brigand statesmen was the destruction of the Temporal Power. For this end the aid of England was necessary. Lord Palmerston, who gave that aid, was kept in power by the votes of Catholic Whig-Liberals. These again were mainly returned to Parliament by the exertions of Cardinal Cullen and the Castle bishops. So that we have here an open, undeniable direct connection between the Irish Castle prelates, and the spoliation of the Pope! Was ever such conjunction seen or heard of since Christianity began? Nor can it be alleged that the Cardinal and the pro-Whig bishops were ignorant of the facts. We learn the contrary from their own confession. When the first attack was made on the Pope, there was a great commotion, and much fine speaking and general make-believe. In Kerry, in particular, a great meeting was held, at which the bishop (Dr. Moriarty), after proving Lord Palmerston's complicity with the revolution, declared: "If our members don't give up Lord Palmerston we shall have to give them up." Alas for Dr. Moriarty's consistency! The members did not give up Lord Palmerston, and the bishop never carried his threat beyond words. The Whig alliance continued and continues active and operative. The interests of the Irish people and the Catholic Church are still bartered for places for Whig lawyers. The Cardinal has never retracted the charge of the Rochefort alliance, though twice explained and denied. Can the alliance of the Castle Bishop be denied or defended?

This it is which has ruined Ireland in our day. This it is which must be for once and for ever ended if the Church in Ireland is to take her rightful place and do the work she only can do in the salvation of the people and the reconstitution of society. Much more has to be said on this point. Much more also on the condition to which the elimination of the national idea from Catholic affairs has reduced religion in Dublin. For the present we must leave the east, and hastening westwards, see to what a state of demoralisation the Catholic Whig-Liberal confederacy is reducing Connaught.

I am, sir, yours,

AN IRISH CATHOLIC LAYMAN.

THE ARCHBISHOP OF TUAM.

SIR,—The precedence due to his rank having been given to his Eminence of Dublin, the great western archdiocese—long associated with everything Catholic and patriotic in Irish affairs—now imperatively claims attention : for there a conspiracy against Ireland is being woven ; there an attempt is being made, the most audacious our day has seen, to restrict, if not to destroy popular liberty.

In the famous letter to Lord Shrewsbury, by which O'Connell relegated that nobleman to private life, he quotes a Jesuit proverb to the effect that "there is no enemy so dangerous to religion as a very pious fool." With a slight change in the terms, we may declare with equal truth that there is no enemy more dangerous to Ireland than a learned, able, astute, pro-Whig bishop. If he be in addition active, zealous and edifying in the discharge of his religious functions, all the worse ; since he gains so much more weight, the better his character.

When dissecting a question of the hour, when the knife at every stroke may wound susceptibilities entitled to respect, or touch elevated persons, the utmost caution is required in the operator. He must be perfectly sure of his ground, that while presuming to censure others, no matter with what excellence of motive, he may not subject himself to merited blame. To this end it is necessary to make anew certain distinctions and provisions.

The Catholic Church, divine in her origin, perfect in her structure, immutable in her principles, immaculate in her life, never stands in need of reformation ; never can be reformed. She is unchangeable, because she is perfect. On the other hand the human element through which and by which she operates in the world has a constant tendency—because it is human, and therefore imperfect—to run into excess, to suffer decay. When reforms are mentioned in relation to the Church, they are not of her essence, but of her accidents. These changes she herself alone can make. They are wrought in His own good time by the Holy Spirit within her. She can never be reformed from without. The laity, whether sovereigns or peoples, cannot have the necessary knowledge, nor have they the right, save in so far as she herself may require their assistance. When, therefore, Catholics observe, as sometimes they must, anything

abnormal in the internal condition of the Church, their place is to wait—
it may be in pain, certainly in patience—till the providential order is
manifested, and the necessary changes are effected from within. In this,
as in many other matters, God's providence is inscrutable, and not to be
probed or fathomed by the slender intelligence of man. With the
internal affairs of the archdiocese of Tuam, therefore, the public have no
right to interfere. The Ordinary may practise his priests in the virtue
of detachment, if he judge it good for their spiritual health; he may
multiply in their regard the seven deadly sins to seventy, and make *ipso
facto* suspensions by the score; he may create a class of "migratory
curates" (as his organ in the press lately called them), and circulate
them from the mountains to the islands—from the Twelve Pins to Clare
and Boffin and the Arrans. With all this the public has nothing to
do, and, if it take a humble advice, it will not concern itself.

Very different should be the conduct of the people when the secular
order is unjustly invaded, and the attempt made to strain the spiritual
authority to the destruction of their lawful freedom. In secular things
they are the judges. The Circular of Propaganda itself declares it has
no intention of dominating in that order. The clergy of the archdiocese
of Tuam may be tongue-tied, and manacled, and fettered. The laity
may lament the loss of their guidance and co-operation—for the priest
is not less but more of a citizen because he is a priest. This they cannot
exclaim against nor help. But when in aid of an infamous Government
and a vicious oligarchy the spiritual power intervenes, to reduce them,
as well as its immediate subjects, to abject silence and ungrateful inaction,
then they are bound to stand forward, not less as Catholics than as
Irishmen, to defend their liberties and meet with stern opposition such a
perversion of authority. To leave abstractions, the Archbishop of Tuam
has not only imposed submission to the Circular on his clergy under the
severest penalties, but he has endeavoured to force it on his people.
During his recent visitations he has put it forward everywhere, declaring
to his people that they are bound to obey the Pope in spirituals *and* in
temporals. Now, on the face of it, this is being more Papal than the
Pope : that is, it is anti-Papal. Excess in teaching may be as harmful
as defect. The Pope, as we know, teaches the supremacy of the spiritual
and temporal orders each in its own sphere. But he by reason of his
spiritual supremacy is judge of the limits of both, and, as a necessary
consequence, is guardian of the freedom of the temporal order as well as
the spiritual. The assertion that he is supreme in both orders is, if it
be seriously maintained, more akin to the orthodoxy of Moscow than of
Rome. Is not this the ground of the charge of the Archbishop's friend
and ally, the author of "Vaticanism," that Catholics can hold no true

allegiance to the Queen because of the prior claim of the Pope? Is this
not also making ground for the chief objections so often urged against
Emancipation? The assertion of this supremacy in both orders for the
Pope will seem incredible to many, but it rests on evidence too strong to
admit of doubt.

It may be said that the Archbishop only "advised," or "was not
properly understood." There is no misunderstanding what follows : In
one place at least the Circular, " which only concerned the bishops, and
had no political bearing "—it was only meant to smother Parnell and all
he represents, and bury them out of sight—has not only been used
against the rights of the clergy as citizens, but forced on the people
with a violence nothing short of scandalous. In one of the principal
towns of the archdiocese, on the feast of SS. Peter and Paul, the incumbent, a dignitary of the chapter, after Mass in place of the Gospel of the
day inveighed against the "busybodies," the "venal scribblers," who
attempted to seduce his people to subscribe to the Parnell Tribute.
They were by the canon's declaration taking the part of the adversaries
of the Church and of the enemy of man against God, &c., &c. The men
thus stigmatised are some of the best Irishmen and Catholics in Connaught. One in particular is widely known. His character, as Christian
and citizen, it would not be easy to match. His voice, and pen, and
purse have ever been at the service of his country, and never has he in
much or in little sought praise or reward therefor. This too was in a
town distinguished for its Catholic spirit, whose people of all others are
prompt to respond to their pastor's call for every good and religious
purpose. Does he imagine his legitimate influence will be increased by
this exhibition of spiritual tyranny? Are they not justified in calling it
a grave abuse of his sacred trust—a desecration of God's altar for a
political purpose as vain as it is base? This must be taken as the work
of the Archbishop, for no priest within his jurisdiction would dare to take
action of the kind without his approval, expressed or implied.

Now what was in question to provoke this unlawful proceeding? No
public meeting, no agitation of any kind, nothing but a whisper, as it
were, among two or three of the principal people of B——, that there
should be some steps taken to fall into line with the rest of the country.
The movement could have been, and in fact was, suppressed by a hint
from the presbytery. This however was not sufficient, and what is here
related followed. It is only one more example of many that, when an
Irish ecclesiastic goes over to the enemy, he loses moderation and judgment with all feeling of sacerdotal propriety.

What has this man Parnell done that his very name should enrage
the West Britons? He did what they did not do—stood between the

people and the workhouse, the emigrant ship and death by famine.
Aristocratic by birth and connections—English, or at least non-Irish, in
breeding, in mental constitution, in everything in fact but his passionate,
absorbing, consuming patriotism—he left his class and order, all the
pleasures and ambitions of life, the certain success and distinction his
abilities would have won him, to give, like our first Liberator, " the
years of his buoyant youth and cheerful manhood" to the service of the
Irish people. And this is his reward from Catholic ecclesiastics !

Whatever of gratitude Ireland owes to him is quadrupled in Mayo ;
and under the " nervous pressure of corruption" Mayo makes no sign.
Barely four years ago he went to Westport and spoke the words which
broke the neck of landlordism before ever land law bound it—words
which will be emblazoned yet in Irish history as those which formulated
the emancipation of Irish industry :—" The famine is on you. Do not,
as you did before, pay rent in November to die of starvation in February.
Keep a grip of the homestead. Pay the people who have fed and clothed
you ; keep provision for the hungry mouths ; if any surplus remain,
give it to the landlord, for it is his." Noble words ! As catholic and
orthodox in the moral order, as they were wise and statesmanlike in
the political, they flashed through Mayo as lightning does ; unlike
lightning, they remained. The serf heard them as a revelation, he stood
upright, and for the first time in his history confronted his tyrant. This
is Parnell's inexpiable sin, " the head and front of his offending."

Time was when Ireland, in doubt, or difficulty, or danger, turned to
the chair of St. Jarlath to hear the word of "light and leading"—the
trumpet sound, always certain. Ireland turns no longer to that venerable
seat. No more is the trumpet heard—happily perhaps, for the only
thing certain about it is that the sound, if it came, would be uncertain.
I do not presume to allege this as a wilful defect. It arises from the
unfortunate fact that the present occupant of that ancient see is
entirely innocent of the science of politics. His ideas thereon vary
with the day or the hour. They are for him matter of the purest
expediency. The only principle he holds in this order, if principle
it be, is that he should be always on the winning side. Of this it may
be remarked that if the Apostles held the same there would be no Christianity in the world to-day. Unhappily for the present Archbishop,
he succeeds a prelate as pre-eminent as a statesman and patriot as
he was a Churchman. For anyone of average merit or capacity the
contrast is crushing. Still more unhappily, the present Administration—
I refer to it only as touching the public order—seems to have one
dominating idea, namely, the reversal of all that during nigh half a
century made Tuam illustrious. Dr. Mac Hale had first in view after

his obligatory duties the preservation and development of the Irish
national spirit, and all that constitutes Irishmen as a distinct family
among the nations.   Dr. M'Evilly seems bent on making his people
West Britons.   On Good Friday the ancient tongue tells no longer to the
people, in such pathetic way as no other could, the tragic story of
Redemption.   The Irish-English catechism is banished from the schools ;
the vicious principle of the National system is being intruded on the
convents, to the exclusion, it must be supposed, of holy symbol and
pious ejaculation.   It is not an extravagant idea that the Christian
Brothers, being intensely Irish and Catholic, may find their position
untenable in the archdiocese, as they have found it elsewhere, and take
wing to a more genial atmosphere, leaving the popular schools void of
the history and religion of the people, to rear a new generation neither
Irish nor Catholic.

In other ways, which it would not be proper to mention here, the
ancient order is being reversed in the archdiocese.   We may imagine
how, under Dr. Mac Hale's sway, the generosity of the West would be
stimulated to pay some portion of the debt due to Mr. Parnell.   We
may imagine how the West would press forward in its newly-found
liberty to emulate more favoured regions in doing its duty.   Now, alas !
there is shame and disorganisation on one hand, on the other the apathy
and stagnation which result in corruption or in secret societies.   If the
Archbishop deigns to cast his eye over these lines, and perchance be
struck with the possibility of their being a true representation of the
state of the archdiocese, if he want further confirmation, let him
assemble his clergy in their deaneries ; let him put them to the issue for
or against his present policy ; let the vote be by ballot, and I will stake
my life he will be astonished at the result.

In any event so astute a prelate cannot remain much longer in doubt
of the situation.   He loves to be on the winning side.   He is now
assuredly on the losing one.   Let us state the position once more.   If
the policy of Dr. Mac Hale was, as Ireland thinks it was, wise and
sagacious, magnanimous and disinterested, Irish and Catholic before all,
the policy of Dr. M'Evilly, which is the contrary of all these, cannot be
other than destructive of the best interests of "faith and fatherland."

He will perchance yet awaken to the fact that archbishops, no more
than humbler people, cannot sit on two stools without the inevitable
catastrophe ensuing ; that it is not in the nature of things to be able to
run with the hare and hunt with the hounds ; and that no Irish
ecclesiastic of high or low degree can exchange confidences and favours
with Dublin Castle and preserve the love and respect of his people.
All Ireland is coming in to join heart and hand in the common intent.

To use again the language of the famous Circular, "it is not to be tolerated" that a new Ulster be made of Connaught, when the old is breaking down on all sides the barrier of prejudice and hate which so long estranged it. The Archbishop may seem to succeed for the moment; he may depend on it, ultimate success in this disastrous way will mean ruin equally for himself and Ireland,

I am, sir, yours,

AN IRISH CATHOLIC LAYMAN.

CARDINAL M'CABE AND THE PAPAL CIRCULAR.

SIR,—With what appears a strange infelicity, his Eminence Cardinal M'Cabe, in replying to the address presented on Sunday, passes from its subject to a defence of the Papal authority and the recent Circular. The address was in itself a perfectly proper and laudable thing, in which his spiritual subjects of all shades of opinion could join. The reply must have given pain to very many present. With some portions of it we may quite agree; others are merely truisms known to every Catholic, and about which there can be no dispute. What is alone worthy of remark is that the Cardinal claims, by implication rather than openly, for the Circular of Propaganda the submission due to a Papal utterance, *ex cathedrâ.*

To his Eminence we willingly pay the homage due to his person and office, second to one only in power and dignity; to his teaching, in the Catholic order, prompt and full acceptance. This is our duty to him. On the other hand, we are entitled, by this very submission, to claim that the teaching shall bear the stamp of infallibility, or be representative of the soundest tradition of Catholic doctrine. We fail to find these notes in some things for which his Eminence contends. Before the Circular can be urged upon our acceptance it must be considerably altered in form. It must show who are the persons—followers of Mr. Parnell—and what the acts condemned. It must take the programme of the Land League and that of the National League, and extract from them the passages asserted to be contrary to Catholic doctrine and Christian morals. In a word, on this all-important matter we require, and we have a right to demand, clear, precise, scientific teaching. When this is offered us we will know our position and our duty. Until then it is perfectly vain to charge men with heresy to whom the barest thought of that sin of sins is abhorrent.

Concluding a hurried letter, I may observe that the Cardinal does not seem to be well served by his Chapter. Is there no member of it

with courage enough to tell him that there are thousands of Catholics
in Dublin, who, God aiding them, would die for the faith, who will not
enter a church when he presides or read a line that he writes? What
can the Castle give to make up for the danger to faith: this state of
things which must eventuate in loss of souls? He asserts a unanimity
amongst the clergy of Dublin which no more obtains than it exists in
the Church in Ireland ; and if his Eminence take the methods humbly
suggested to the Archbishop of Tuam, he will ascertain the fact with a
completeness which, I venture to say, will rival the western archdiocese.

AN IRISH CATHOLIC LAYMAN.

GALWAY AND ELPHIN.

SIR,—So many "highways, paths, and byways" (to quote poor
Mangan's ringing line) open from the road we are travelling, that there
is some danger of the guide losing himself, or at least wearying his
followers by straying into their tempting though not flowery ways. At
some risk of the latter contingency, I must return to Galway, as the
picture (at best necessarily an imperfect one) drawn in a previous letter
would otherwise be wanting in some of its strongest tints.

History is made rapidly nowadays. Events of the first magnitude
crowd quickly on each other. The wonder of to-day is forgotten to-
morrow. But as the highest mountain, eclipsed by the nearness of its
lesser fellows, stands out as we recede in distance, so the cardinal facts
of human history, as time flows on, take their true place and become the
landmarks of succeeding ages. One of these facts I take to be the late
Ladies' Land League. Appearing at a crisis of greatest peril, it did its
intended work with wonderful success, and—this ended—as became its
constituents, disappeared as modestly and quietly as it rose.

The most thorough advocate of English rule must now confess that
the suppression of the Land League was an unlawful, as time has proved
it to be an impolitic, measure. We may not wonder at this, for Government cares as little for law or justice as a Castle bishop cares for the
canons when he has some personal end in view. In this connection how
often are we reminded of what this dignitary seems careful to forget—
the injunction of the Apostle, that "Bishops should not lord it over
Christ's heritage." But this by the way. Ministers had shortly before
declared in Parliament that the L.L. was a lawful organization. It had
not changed its programme or principles or methods in any way when it
was proclaimed. The conclusion therefore is inevitable—that the high-

handed act was not due to any fault of the League, but to the intrigues of the landlords and the brutal temper of the Chief Secretary.

It suited the latter to charge it with inciting to crime. He will never be able to justify his arrest of Michael Davitt, when the latter returned from America for the avowed purpose of preaching a crusade against violence of all kinds.

The foundation of the Ladies' Land League on the suppression of the other bears all the marks of a providential inspiration. The movement was in a most critical state. If the land monopolists succeeded in breaking down the popular spirit they might have prevented even the present sham settlement operating. Like their sisters at the Siege of Limerick, the women of the League rushed to the breach and defended the walls when the men were struck down. For nigh two years they bore the brunt of the struggle with virile strength and womanly tact. Nothing more singular, more effectual, more beneficent has been seen in our day than the work of those women. Wholly without training in business or public affairs, they administered an enormous fund with wonderfully few mistakes. Penetrating everywhere, they sustained the popular spirit; really, though not nominally, carried on the movement; and in thousands of cases prevented or relieved the ravages of landlordism.

One of the tests of the success of the L. L. L. was the virulence with which it was assailed. All the organs and influences of landlordism did their worst in invective and denunciation. To aid his friends came his Eminence of Dublin, who fulminated against the League in such fashion as to compel the unexampled return of a public rebuke from a brother prelate. Nor here should be omitted a note of gratitude to A. M. Sullivan, who took the Irish Catholic side with a power entirely his own.

Perhaps the very worst examples of Irish landlordism are to be found in the county of Galway; and the three which should be placed first in bad pre-eminence have women for actors. With one of these the name of Carraroe will be associated till the doomed institution with its iniquities and consequent crimes will be forgotten in the prosperity of a new Ireland.

To cope with the evils bred by the devilish system, a strong branch of the L. L. L. was formed in Galway. It had not time to begin its work when, following the example of Cardinal M'Cabe, Dr. M'Evilly inveighed against it with such force as to scatter it beyond recall. I will not ask you, sir, to record the epithets—more derogatory to his own dignity and the holy place from which he spoke than injurious to them— which he applied to women who were at least respectable, and who certainly meant well.　Two only had the courage to stand against the storm, and on these fell the local work of the League, besides the attending to the wants of nigh one hundred suspects whom the genial "Buckshot" had immured in Galway jail.　The external work of the branch was not heavy, for, so great was the terrorism exercised, that the clergy with one or two noble exceptions declined to co-operate, nor would they even answer inquiries as to cases of distress in their respective parishes.

Meanwhile the land war in Carraroe went on.　To understand what this meant Carraroe itself must be known, or rather seen.　A sterile waste of rock and sand, with spaces of bog between, if any farmer in the world, besides a native, were offered 500 acres in fee, he would fly from the fatal gift, for on it he would starve.　On this barren territory hundreds of persons were in the course of the struggle threatened with death by famine or exposure.　Literally to save life, Michael Davitt and Ada Yeates went down : the former with money and experience, the latter with skill and devotion.　They not only succeeded in averting the threatened horrors, but they laid the foundation of an industry which promises to raise the people from perennial want to something like comfort.　This is not the place to write the history of Carraroe.　When it is written, Miss Yeates's name will be honoured as few can be ; for few indeed there are whose self-sacrifice would be equal to living in a mud hut, not for days or months, but years, to lift out of misery Connemara peasants.　And this, and much more, this gently-nurtured, highly-educated lady has done.

The point of the example is this.　For the wealthy owner claiming a rent never earned from the land,* and using the utmost rigour of the

---

* For the benefit of those who do not know the western seaboard from Donegal to Kerry it may be well to say that the rents exacted are rarely (if ever) for value in land, but are made up by fishing, kelp-making, and any other industry open to the people.　They are in reality serfs, whose labour is taxed by their owners.　One notorious landlady in Galway exacts first the highest rent for the mountain and bog which she lets her slaves ; she then taxes the sand of the shore (which is common property), the shellfish they gather, the sea-wrack they risk life to collect, and the turbary, which was formerly free.　She would tax also the light and air of heaven and the running streams, if they were not beyond her.　And to enforce these monstrous exactions the Government granted her, free, the forces of the Crown, with police and Emergency men !　And her tenants are not happy !　Stupid tenants ! ungrateful Irish !　Within sight of Carraroe an extensive eviction took place at the same time as the attempted evictions in that place.　A large number, I think as many as eighty families, were put out of their wretched homes.　Their united possessions in food and furniture would not, supposing them saleable at all, bring £5.　Their condition was so utterly wretched, so hopelessly destitute, that the officers of the marines, the sub-inspectors, the men engaged, to the last of the constabulary, made a collection, which amounted to £10, for the temporary relief of the starving people.　This eviction, from the remoteness of the locality (it can only be approached by sea) was not known to the public, nor commented on in the press, and the perpetrator of the fearful tragedy escaped the reprobation which he deserved.　He has not, however, escaped the land courts, which in many instances have cut down his rents *sixty* per cent.

law to enforce it, Dr. M'Evilly had no word of public remonstrance or censure, though she lives in his immediate neighbourhood and is subject in every respect to his jurisdiction. For the people of Carraroe no public manifestation of sympathy or call for aid. For those who assisted them in the hour of sorest need nothing but hard words. The wretched Carraroe peasant and his wife and children might go to the poorhouse (as they did go to Oughterard), and get mocked for their pains ; or they might take to the emigrant ship, which was not there ; or they might starve quietly, as they did before; or end suffering and life together in Galway Bay—let what might happen to the *miserables*, the serene tranquillity of Mrs.——, of——, must not be disturbed. To put it in plainest language, what does this mean ? It is not only the abandonment of the flock by the shepherd to worse than lupine ravage, but the assailing of those who took up and performed the lapsed duty with the most undeserved and unjust reproaches.

So much for Tuam. If any person who may have read these letters be still incredulous, enough remains behind to prove to demonstration that the policy followed by the present Archbishop most efficiently seconds the Government in its efforts to ruin the Irish nation.

Not without reluctance do I approach the last individual example it is necessary at present to give of the "stone-blind" or Castle or West-British policy ; for it is impossible to approach the Bishop of Elphin without a feeling of personal respect. Dr. Gillooly is no common man. On other lines he is capable of doing a work for Ireland only second to that of Dr. McHale in the past and Dr. Croke in the present. Unfortunately for himself and country he goes in every public matter hopelessly wrong. Of great abilities and attainments, of austere virtues, of uncommon energy of character and strength of will—in fine, with most of the qualities, the aggregate of which justly entitles their possessor to be called "great"—he could have taken a foremost part and done invaluable work in building up the national autonomy on true and enduring lines. As it is, he has frittered away on most worthless objects, a character which would have ranked him with the foremost of Irish Churchmen, and opportunities for good which will never return. It is a thousand pities, for there is something sterling and honest in his nature which does not allow him to appear other than he is. No claim makes he to patriotism. He is with the aristocracy and the Government, and he does not deny it. He moves amongst his priests and people with as (apparently) profound an indifference to their feelings, opinions, and interests, as if he were Emperor of China or Mikado of Japan. Consequently he has lost, and it must be confessed justly, all political influence with both. He makes mistakes which the least acquaintance with his

people would enable him to avoid, and brings his authority to naught
by commanding when they will not obey.   For example, at the last
election of Roscommon he issued a circular to the clergy obliging them
to recommend the O'Conor Don to the electors.   It was said at the time
that one of the most efficient causes of the Don's rejection was this
circular.   At the last Sligo election the bishop's selections were D. M.
O'Conor and Colonel King-Harman.   The former has passed from the
judgment of men.   With a sincere prayer for his soul's repose I will
say only of him what duty requires.   He was a man who utterly belied
all the expectations formed of him—and they were high.   He was capable
of much ; he did nothing : and he failed because he was a West-British
Whig.   If a wooden image had been placed on the bench of the
House of Commons and labelled "Sligo," it would have done as good
service as Denis M. O'Conor during the present Parliament.   It
has been said he was long ill.   Why did he not resign and permit
another to do the duty he could not fulfil ?   The Don of course
wanted his vote to force his own claims on the Ministry.   As to the
colonel, the bishop's other candidate, it is enough to say that, if you
reproduced his portrait as painted by himself during the recent contest
in Dublin, you would run a good chance of being indicted for libel.
These are the men for whom the Bishop of Elphin turned his back on
Thomas Sexton.

One more example of the bishop's "loss of touch " of his people.
When the Land Act was passed through, he contributed nothing towards
its passing, but rather the reverse ; he came out with a scheme for its
working through parish committees.   A circular was read embodying
the proposal, and the priests were directed to hold meetings and begin
the organisation.   Not one single committee was formed.   One priest
put it before his people in this fashion :   " Here is a circular the bishop
commands me to read.   I do so under obedience.   You can act as you
like regarding it."   And the people did so, and let it alone.   The fact is
there is not a bogtrotter in Sligo or Roscommon will cross the road
(political) at his bishop's bidding.

There is a peculiar suitability in recalling the position just now.
The bishop confidently predicted the triumph of the Don in Wexford.   If
the latter is not taught by defeat, he will predict with equal confidence
his victory in Sligo, with a still more disastrous result.   Castle bishops
never learn ; nor do I think there is on record a single instance of their
conversion to Irish ideas.

There is something exceedingly fortunate in the Wexford election.
The Don went down in piebald fashion—not black and white, but blue and
orange.   In this contest he got so plucked and bedraggled that his

cousin, the jackdaw of Rheims, would not acknowledge him. It is impossible that a constituency which is favoured with Sexton's priceless services will tolerate the address of "the last of the Whigs," sent back from Wexford in such scarecrow fashion.

With this I leave, sir, the ungracious though necessary task of declaiming against the hostility of those who should be neutral, if not with us; and, returning to the general question, will endeavour to point out the causes which have led to the present situation, with such hints as these may suggest for its amelioration.

Yours truly,

An Irish Catholic Layman.

NEGLECTED DUTIES.

Sir,—If my humble voice could reach every man within our bounds capable of thinking and acting as an Irishman and a Catholic, the question I would put to him is this: " How long shall the Castle bishop be permitted to traverse every public movement, and aid our adversaries in preventing the fruition of the nation's hopes?" The enemy before us we can guard against and overcome; the mistaken or false friend in our camp makes our chief danger. This is a question not to be lightly considered or carelessly answered. Leaving my readers to ponder it well, satisfied that a proper solution will be found in good time, I will now proceed to substantiate the three counts of the indictment stated in a former letter.

These were: That the West-British bishop failed in his duty as a guardian of Catholic education, as a patriot, and as a Catholic publicist. Taking the last count first, we must revert to the real starting-point of the present situation.

It has been said before, it cannot be too often insisted on, that the work before the Church in Ireland, when the Act of Emancipation struck the fetters from her limbs, was second only to that presented to the infant Church on its emergence from the Catacombs. Leaving for the moment the remoter object of the restoration of the empire to the unity of Christendom—now alas! little more than the "shadow of a great name"— she had here to reform and refound society on a just and Christian basis; she had to bring the law of the land in the particulars most essential to the well-being of society into conformity with the law of God. For Ireland, then as now intensely Catholic as regards the faith of the masses of the people, is Protestant, Pagan, anti-Christian, or anything

you like but Catholic, as regards the constitution of society, and the set
and current of public opinion. At this day, two generations after
Emancipation, there is hardly any Catholic public opinion properly so
called. There is no Catholic society—that is, there is in the centres of
population no number of people of various classes drawn together by
Catholic principles for Catholic objects, which I take to be the body and
essence of Catholic social life. There is, indeed, something in the larger
cities which is called "Catholic" society, but it is dominated by a
vulgar, snobbish, non-Catholic spirit. It is full of worldliness and
ostentation. It is wholly wanting in the simplicity, good sense, and
charity, of really Catholic society. It is essentially anti-Irish, or, at
least, West-British, and in Dublin has the "Castle" for the chief object
of its devotion. Those who know anything of our principal cities will
grant the truth of this description. The barest acquaintance with what
are called the "better classes" elsewhere—the country gentry and
professional people—discloses a still lower state. Their nearly
total want of literary culture, the poverty and tenuity of
their intellectual life, their want of robust Catholic spirit,
make any union for Irish or Catholic objects impossible. The
conversation of the men is confined to the price of cattle, the betting
on the next race, or some grand jury or poor law jobbery; their reading
does not extend beyond the daily paper. The women talk of the fashions
or the latest scandal, and read "Ouida's" novels. Of such is better class
Catholic society in Catholic Ireland. But this is digressing. The first
duty of the Catholic hierarchy, when its action was free, was to enforce
on the Government the primal law of any society which aims at progress,
namely, the protection of industry from unjust spoliation. That "the
labourer is worthy of his hire," that "the husbandman shall first partake
of the fruits," are conclusions of reason as well as first principles of justice.
For if the labourer be not paid his hire he cannot labour long; if the
husbandman do not eat he cannot live. So far, the Irish landlord yielded
to necessity; he permitted his serfs to retain as much as kept them
living, and enabled them to work for him; beyond that, not, if he could
help it, a shilling nor a meal. We talk of periodical famines, and the
great famine; in vast tracts of Ireland, famine is perennial. To end this
infamy—this sin of the governing class calling to heaven for vengeance—
was clearly the most urgent work before the bishops. For if their first
duty was to teach their people the way to heaven, their second was to
prevent their being sent on the way before their time. If the bishop
have no flock to teach he may be bishop no longer. St. Paul himself
could found no Christian State on a horde of half-starved serfs. The Irish
landlord, having the legislative and executive powers in his hands, framed

a code of laws, which made rack-renting and evicting the normal conditions of Irish agricultural industry. His ally, the English Government, had previously stamped out nearly every other; so that the people, nominally emancipated, were practically condemned to an industrial serfdom which made progress and contentment impossible. So scandalously unjust, so utterly indefensible, was the Irish land system, that, although it was regarded as the outwork of the land monopoly of Great Britain, and had the force of the empire at its back, it went down, at the stern challenge of the "ex-convict" (as his enemies delight to call the founder of the League), with hardly a show of resistance.

Were it not for the Castle bishop, the Irish Church would have done fifty years ago, what the League did but yesterday, and we would have now a flourishing, highly organised society of ten or twelve millions, instead of a disorganised and perishing one of half the number. He saw, or might have seen, the rackrenting and evicting. He saw his people, and he sees them yet, condemned to conditions of food and clothing and lodging, unfit for the beasts that perish; he saw the law-made famines and exterminations, and he not only did nothing himself, but he opposed the action of those who would have done everything, for the good providence of God has provided that in the Irish Church there should be at every period bishops as conspicuous for their patriotism as for the highest episcopal virtues. Let us, however, be just to this thrice-unhappy personage, the Castle bishop. He is the outcome and evidence of an evil time. He was probably born a serf, or is certainly the son of one; and the servile strain is not eliminated in one generation. Then mark the temptation to which he was subjected. One day the despised head of a persecuted sect; the next the chief of an emancipated people—a peer among peers, with vastly greater influence than any peer of them all. No wonder some bishops lost their heads; no wonder they abused powers to which they were wholly unused; no wonder they forgot that Ireland was a missionary country, in which the Christian order had to be created from the foundation, and entered at once into the state and mode of life proper to prelates of countries where it had existed for centuries. Nor did they always escape the taint of the non-Catholic, anti-Irish feeling, common to the aristocratic society of which they were made free. The late Dr. Moriarty was one of the most accomplished prelates who ever adorned the Irish Church; from him everything of good might have been anticipated; but when he entered the *salons* of Kenmare House he was lost to Ireland and the Church; and did and said things which, in charity to his memory, we may not recall. In another way it is remembered with bitterness in Tipperary how, during the reign of Dr. Leahy, the elections for the county were made at the Palace in Thurles in total

E

indifference to the rights of the electors. Usurping popular power, he made himself sole elector. Happily we may refer to this as a thing of the past, for the great spiritual chief of Munster to-day is not only of one mind and heart with his people, but is scrupulously regardful of their rights.

"But," the Castle bishop may object, "it is not my business to interfere in secular matters ; I could not inaugurate a movement to effect a change in the laws." With great respect, the duty of the bishop as regards the good of his charge in the temporal as well as the spiritual order is only bounded by his power. Besides, the right of the people to live by their industry is not merely a secular matter : it is essentially a moral one, coming quite within episcopal duty and power to secure. Then as to enforcing reform, the means were entirely in his own hand. I have pointed them out before. It was simply making the unwritten and manifestly just law of the League operative through every parish of his diocese—namely, that no one should take a farm evicted for non-payment of an unjust rent, and that no one should speak to or have any transaction with anyone who did. A Tenants' Defence Association in every parish, with the *parochus* for president or secretary, enforcing these simple laws, would have made an end of landlordism long before it had time to reduce Ireland to its present state of impoverishment and degradation.

It is only when we take the highest view of the great office to which he is called that we see how utterly the Castle bishop has failed in his duty as publicist—that is, as one who connects Catholic principles with the external order. Once more let it be declared that the Catholic Church is no sect among the sects, no school of philosophy, but a power, a kingdom, with a sovereignty of its own, no less real and true because unseen. It is the practical providence of God to men, for when its action is free, and its human elements worthy, its effect is to establish a condition of society in which the ordinary evils and miseries which afflict mankind are unknown. Though the immediate mission of the Church is to the souls of men, it embraces mediately their temporal interests. It is at once general and particular, spiritual and material. Its effect is to show forth in society the Divine sentence, "Seek ye first the kingdom of God, and his justice, and *all* things shall be added to you." In raising the individual to the primal integrity and perfection of his nature, it restores society to that happy condition which we know to be possible, but which is so rare in the world's history. Under the Jewish theocracy we read of the people dwelling in peace, "each man under his own vine and fig-tree, no one daring to make him afraid." For three centuries Ireland presented a still more beautiful picture, in as far as the Christian order surpassed the Jewish. The legend embodied by the poet in graceful song,* if not historically exact, is evidence of a condition of society in the highest degree honourable to the Ireland of that time; while the reception and support of thousands of students in quest of the learning which had found its chief refuge here, proves that abundance dwelt with peace and virtue in our isle. Under Alfred England likewise showed the power of Catholic principles in creating a society approaching perfection. So likewise under St. Louis in France, and Ferdinand and Isabella in Spain; while it was reserved for the great Society of Jesus in the missions of Paraguay to exhibit the highest state which human society is capable of attaining. There the law of charity reigned supreme, there the sacred tribunal of penance was the only one known; and human law with its rude methods and practical injustices was wholly superseded by the divine.

It is the highest praise which can be given our people to declare that never before was fairer field offered for the exhibition of the power and beneficence of Catholic principles. The faith through centuries of persecution had become, as it were, ingrained in the national life. The organisation of the Church remained almost complete; she had only to frame the necessary laws for the establishment of justice in the public order, and the whole framework of injustice melted away before it, as,

> " When torches that have burned all night
> At some impure and Godless rite
> Encounter morning's glorious rays."

The late Land League is evidence. It was improvised in a chance, haphazard way; its methods were untried, and some of its instruments unworthy. Yet, as Forster bitterly confessed, its unwritten law superseded the law of the land. It did so because it was the reflection of eternal justice, and had a true and loyal people for its subjects. In truth and fact it cannot be too often repeated there is no height of devotion and self-sacrifice to which this people cannot be raised for Irish and Catholic objects if the leading be honest and capable. In spite of much to try it their faith is still a living and zealous faith. Missionaries of widest experience are filled with admiration of it. I have been many times told by these masters of the spiritual life that they have frequently found the people more willing to follow than their chiefs to lead. If anyone wants evidence of this, let him go to the nearest country church and see in the rapt, profound devotion of the people, their utter absence of human respect, and freedom from any thought but of the one tremendous action passing—a sight more edifying than the most eloquent discourse—a proof of their undying, invincible attachment to the principles by which nations as well as

---

* " Rich and rare were the gems she wore."

individuals live. The Irish people are willing and eager to be led on Irish and Catholic lines. The Castle bishop cannot retire under the question asked of old, "Am I my people's keeper?" He had the power and the right, he had the material to work with, he had the duty upon him. The first he did not use, the second he permitted to be wasted and abused, the last he wholly neglected.

It is not yet too late, while the advance of political intelligence and the growth of a certain independence of spirit make delays dangerous. The Irish people will gladly be led by their spiritual chiefs, but the leading must be on the old lines, and for public objects. Once more : they will *not* be led through the mire of Whiggery, nor into the shadow of Dublin Castle.

I am, sir, yours, &c.,

AN IRISH CATHOLIC LAYMAN.

THE CASTLE BISHOP AS A PATRIOT.

SIR,—When this series of letters was projected I expected in return, not argument—for in answer to the statement of the Irish position nothing is thinkable which could be justified by that name— but a good deal of obloquy. Writing anonymously and with one single aim, this would not have touched me ; but I am nevertheless obliged to your correspondent, "An Irish Catholic Clergyman," for experience of a pleasanter kind. The answer to his courteous letter comes within the scope of the present, and I beg leave to assure him that he curiously mistakes my relations with bishops. It has been my happiness during a third of a century to have known many, to be intimate with several, and to be honoured with the friendship of more than one. Never once have I approached one of the rulers of God's Church without experiencing courtesy and kindness beyond deserving, nor asked favour which was refused. As to the graver charge of lessening the popular respect for ecclesiastics, my design is to increase it by stigmatising a course of action on the part of some which can have only that unhappy result.

One of the most beautiful traits in the Irish character is its profound instinctive reverence for the priestly office. It is ingrained in the national life, the outcome of a vivid faith, and rooted in true and deep theology. The Great Briton jeers and mocks at this feeling. He loves to scoff at "Paddy and his priest." It could not be otherwise. The Saxon lout with his grossness of temperament and swinish habit is incapable of understanding the mingled respect and affection which bind in one the Irish Church and people. This is no outcome of slavish fear or abject superstition, but of life-long benefits on one side, and loyal support and obedience springing from an intimate sense of the value and dignity of the priestly office on the other.   The Irish peasant sees in the priest his sole friend, his defence against injustice, his protector against the multiplied oppressions to which he was subject.   More, he sees in him the representative of Jesus Christ, " whose mouth opens in benediction," whose hand is extended to raise and to save.   Instead of lessening, I would make this feeling dominant in Irish affairs.   I would restore to the Church her mediæval power, but I would have it used for the purpose for which it was conferred.   I would make her in the most potent manner the shield of the oppressed, the father of the poor.   I would have her withstand the tyrant, and smite him with the anathema which has never lost its force.   I would have her stand for justice and right against fraud and falsehood and wrong, no matter whether practised by nobles or governments.   I would that the Pope were, as of old, chief of a Christian world, arbiter between sovereigns, and that bishop and parochus, each in his own place, were, as he often is and always might be, for his people the practical Providence of God.

When the first principles of the Christian order have become so obscured that bishops and revolutionists join in crying, " No priests in politics," it may be useful to state them here, though it looks like copying a page of the catechism.

When in the fulness of time the Creator willed the salvation of His creatures and the restoration of human society to its primal perfection, He took to Himself our human nature, and declared that His delight was to be with the children of men.   It was necessary that this stupendous fact, this ineffable desire, should have a home and an expression adequate and worthy ; and the result was the creation of the Catholic Church.   Its ultimate meaning is the dwelling of God amongst men—His being perpetually exposed for their adoration, and His communication to them in the form He has assumed.

Sole perfection in a world of imperfection—sole unimpaired structure in a wilderness of ruins—shrine of her Creator, destined to co-operate with Him in a work greater than creation itself—it was fitting that she should be endowed with all the immunities, privileges, and powers necessary to the fulfilment of her mission.   Well may she declare, to apply in another sense the words of one of her noblest sons—

> "To raise me was the task of Power Divine,
>   Supremest Wisdom, and Primeval Love,"

for in this grandest manifestation of the omnipotence of God the power of the Father, the wisdom of the Son, and the charity of he Holy Spirit are displayed in their highest perfection.   To her has been confided the guardianship of the Incarnate Word, with the fortunes and the happiness of men; and with these sublime trusts were given corresponding powers. "All power," says our Lord, "is given to Me"—that is, as man, since as God He was always Omnipotent. "As my Father sent Me, so I send you." That is, all the power He received as Saviour He delegated to His Church. It could not be otherwise, since it would be contrary to the wisdom of God to impose duties without enabling their fulfilment. Granting therefore that the mission of the Church extends to the creation and development of the Christian order in society, I claim for its chiefs the powers and rights necessary for its fullest performance, and for the Pope the definition of the point when they begin and end; I claim them by reason of the mission she has received, by the principles she embodies, and by the work she has done and still does. If any further definitions be asked for, I claim for the Church the duty and right of doing all the good in her power. In this direction her action has the possible for its boundary.

What we call Christendom was purely the work of the Church—the outcome of her teaching and the fruit of her labour. Not only has she over this the natural rights of creator and the delegated authority of God, but to a certain extent the very rights of God Himself living and reigning within her. These rights and powers are not the less but the more real that they mostly spring from and operate in the supernatural order, have conscience for their domain, and act in ways different from the secular power. When the Church and the secular power are in harmony society is happy and progressive. When they are in antagonism—that is, when the temporal order oppresses or degrades the spiritual—then public order is broken, and society inevitably declines.

This digression, however tedious, is necessary to show the position held of right by the Catholic bishop. He is set for the raising of human society to the Christian ideal. His noble task is to make truth and justice prevail in human affairs. His office is in the highest degree fiduciary, and the trusts are the chief interests not only of men but of God. He does not exist for himself. The purple he wears is not only the emblem of his dignity but the memento of the sacrifice—of his life if necessary—to which he is bound. Writing of Catholics to Catholics there is in this nothing of my own but the statement, as short as I could make it, of what I have received as the Church's teaching, or understand as the outcome of her principles. Now, my objection to the Castle bishop* is this, that he

* My kindly critic takes exception to the phrase "Castle" bishop. I beg leave to remind him that the epithet does not make but only denotes the fact. If it be that the title is felt to be a discredit and a reproach, why does the bishop go to the Castle? I sometimes wonder if he knows how this is regarded by his people. They may continue to respect his person and reverence his office; they all the more regard his

seems to forget or put aside all such considerations. His beneficent powers are not only unused for their proper ends, but perverted, as far as may be without wholly abandoning his position, to the service of the enemy. The danger and the evil of this is not in the frank declaration of it, but in the doing. Better far say out what is in people's minds than let such feelings rankle and fester till they make a schism, as often they have made in other times and places. Let not the "Irish Catholic Clergyman" be afraid. My ardent desire is to make Catholic principles dominate in Irish affairs, and, going by far higher sanction than my own poor judgment, I am doing what one humble man—not, as you know, "experienced or able," but rather the contrary—may do to hasten that consummation.

I proceed, then, to show that lamentable as has been the defect of the Catholic bishop as a Catholic publicist, his failure as a patriot has been still more conspicuous and complete. However strictly the bishop may be bound in other times and places to take the side of justice and right, his obligation in Ireland was intensified beyond comparison. Of old, when warring Europe went to fight, wherever the quarrel began, it was sure to be ended in Flanders. So in the ceaseless struggle of principles which goes on in the world Ireland seems to be the chosen battle-ground for those most strongly opposed. Here are antagonised in a way seen nowhere else the strife of truth and falsehood, justice and injustice, right and wrong, good and evil. The two sides are divided with a clearness seen nowhere else; and the parties to the struggle are each worthy of their cause.

On one side is the Irish nation; on the other that malific power which for seven centuries has compassed its ruin. Nothing can be more clear, definite, and emphatic than the position of the parties in this contest of eight centuries. So many interests go to obscure the facts underlying the whole position that it is necessary to restate it constantly. One of the most strongly marked of the families of peoples into which Providence has cast mankind exists on Irish soil, and has existed from time immemorial. They have a right to live their own life within their own borders. This right has been always denied them; and not only have they not been governed for

---

policy with indignation and abhorrence. Here is a description of his class which I would not venture to make, but which is of far higher, even episcopal, authority : "An English Whig is bad, an Irish Whig is worse, an Irish Catholic Whig is worst of all ; but an Irish ecclesiastical Catholic Whig is —— itself." Let the reader fill the blank for himself—he can't err on the side of strength—and the quotation will be complete. The "I. C. C." reproaches me with not writing on secret societies, the payment of trade debts, &c. It is no just objection to a man who sets before himself a definite task of clear and urgent necessity that he does not undertake to do several other things quite beside his purpose.

their own benefit, but their rulers have been engaged in one ceaseless
conspiracy for their corruption or extermination.   The whole catalogue
of crime has been exhausted by the English Government in Ireland; and
its guilt is intensified by the hypocritical pretences with which it is
carried on.   Beginning in fraud and hypocrisy; concealed for long by
enormous and systematic lying, the facts are now being laid bare to the
world.   The population reduced to one half, and that half, in temper at
least, always within "measurable distance of rebellion;" the rich plains
covered with cattle, and bleak mountain sides dotted with huts not fit
for savages; the poverty constantly increasing with the decrease of the
population; on all sides the roofless cottage, the ruined villa, the deserted
mansion; and with these every feature of neglect, dilapidation, and
decay.   This is the outcome of foreign government, and this is what the
Castle bishop calls on us to endure.   Then there is Lord Derby's
famous declaration that "it would pay us to spend millions in emigrating
this people."   Let us hope he will be "emigrated" before his plan is
reduced to practice.   Again, there is Mr. Trevelyan's "pinch of hunger"
policy, which was to force the sufferers to vacate the cottage they could
re-enter never more.   These and ten thousand other facts prove to
demonstration that the English Government never acquired an equitable
right to govern us, for it never sought our good.   They prove too that
this Government in administration or executive never touches us save
in an adverse or hostile manner.   The English Government never
intended that a prosperous, powerful, Irish Catholic people should
flourish on Irish soil, and they are as far from intending it now as one
or three or seven centuries ago.

They would not if they could, and they could not if they would,
govern us justly.   There are three invincible obstacles to their right
government of this country : first, natural prejudice, massed and intensified by generations of slanderers; secondly, trade jealousy, which has
led England to the commission of some of its greatest crimes; and,
thirdly, sectarian malice, the spirit of the world, and diabolism energising
in these.   Dublin Castle, their representative here, is a ring of
Orangeism and Freemasonry, which is Antichrist in the concrete; and it
can no more act justly or fairly or honestly by us than the Enemy of
man can desire our spiritual good.

With this Godless tyranny—the incarnation of everything infamous
in government—the Castle bishop has allied himself.   He has done what
Pius the Ninth emphatically and indignantly declined to do—"come to
terms with modern civilisation."   He has done this in open violation of
his duty as a patriot, for to the episcopal office belongs specially this noblest
of natural virtues.   The quality of paternity is the highest the Creator

can share with the creature; and the bishop is father above all. Especially is he the guardian and protector of the poor, the weak, and the suffering; and wherever their interests or claims call him he is bound to go. In a time of imminent peril the Castle bishop has not stirred hand or foot, voice or pen, in aiding the struggles of millions of his countrymen for bare life. Nay, he has gone with their enemies, and justified and praised the most vicious Government this century has seen. With exceeding appropriateness of time and place, Dr. McCormack, of Anchonry, on Sunday last, in Galway, drew, with masterly hand, the portrait of the patriot bishop. Well he might, for he was unconsciously painting his own. He had only to look—if such a thought was possible to him—on his own character and career, his intense patriotism and constant readiness to sacrifice himself for his people, to find there what he was putting in words before the newly-consecrated prelate. Well may we hope that this new father of the Church, great as he is in every sense, will surpass in word and work the admirable model placed before him.

Much more might be added, if need was, to show that the West-British bishop utterly fails in his duty in the public order. The enormous powers—and they can hardly be exaggerated—inherent in his great office, are either unused, or used against his people, to the detriment of religion and the imminent danger of the faith. He had the opportunity of founding in Ireland a Christian democracy which would be a wonder and a model to the world. He preferred to lend his powers to sustain an effete aristocracy perishing through its utter worthlessness, and the most infamous Government the civilised world has known. For the present we will leave this view of his lapses to consider what has been his conduct in the all-important matter of education.

I am, sir, yours, &c.,

AN IRISH CATHOLIC LAYMAN.

THE CASTLE BISHOP AS EDUCATOR.

SIR,—Conspicuous and disastrous as has been the failure of the Castle bishop as publicist and patriot, it does not compare in nature or magnitude with his lapse as guardian and representative of Catholic education. To repeat, this man of temporise and compromise, wanting in courage, consistency, and principle, intervened in the Irish movement, after Emancipation, to barter away the better half of its fruits. Entering on a field of victory which he rather retarded than helped to gain, he deprived it, by his unpardonable weakness, of its chief result. Grateful

for toleration—most odious of words when applied to Irish affairs—
oblivious of or indifferent to the nature of the matter in question, he
hastened to make the most favourable terms for his friends of the Pale,
and condemned Ireland to another half century of martyrdom.

In this, as we shall see further on, he touched, if he did not
pass, the very verge of heresy—at least, he whittled away Catholic
principles on this momentous question until they became obscured or
perverted. It is owing to him that the Irish people is not now showing
the world the incomparable results of Catholic education. It is his fault
that the moment they have secured the right to live on their own soil
without being subject to being robbed or imprisoned, starved or
"emigrated," at the caprice of their masters, they will have still before
them the weighty task of reconstructing their whole educational system,
from *National* school to Royal University, and waiting for a generation
for the results. It is wholly due to the confusion of thought, even
amongst Catholics, his defection has caused, that it has become necessary
to recite the very alphabet of a science which should be patent to everyone
who can claim the Catholic name, and be in operation here for more than
half a century.

The Catholic Church, in reconstructing human society in the
Christian order, founds it on the family, the priest, and the school.
Each of these is necessary to the other; without the active co-operation
of the three, Christian society cannot progress, nor, indeed, continue to
exist. The first, on which so much might be said, we must dismiss with
the remark, that our Lord, in dealing with it, only restored it to its
original unity, while, by sanctifying it, and comparing it with His own
mystic union with His Church, He made it worthy to be the corner-stone
of Christian civilisation.

The priest! How shall we who know him speak of him as we feel
without appearing to exaggerate? The Saviour of our nation, our pride,
our hope, the teacher of doctrine, the example of morals, the standard
of conduct, the salt of society—wanting His devotion and self-sacrifice
the Irish people would long ere this have perished off the face of the earth
sunk into the condition of a horde of savages more degraded than Kaffir
or Zulu. To those who accept his mission, his very presence is a sermon.
He diffuses around him an aroma of holiness; like his Master, he blesses
as he passes by. Among ourselves we sometimes give him the "hard"
word," but it is because our ideal of his character is so high that nothing
less than the angelic could reach it. Anyone in the world living the
ordinary life of a priest would be considered a saint. With the exception
of a few (becoming fewer every day) ancient pro-Whigs—born serfs, and
reared in an atmosphere of slavery—the Irish priest is now more than

ever zealous, self-sacrificing, patriotic, ready to lead his people to victory. He holds them in the hollow of his hand, and is able to acquire for them every concession of justice and right—if he were allowed.

There remains the school. Here I should pause, and, with well-founded distrust, desire that some more suitable and more competent hand should deal with this question of questions, this subject of vital and pressing interest. At this moment, the world over, the conflict of civilisation with barbarism, of Christianity with paganism, of virtue and vice, good and evil, rages round the school. Both sides (everyone, apparently, but the Castle bishop) recognise the fact, that to him who dominates in the school the future of the world belongs; that as this is Christian or pagan, so will society necessarily be.

Now, the Catholic Church asserts—has always asserted—her right to dominate in the school. After the necessary dogmas of religion there is no part of her teaching more clear and peremptory than this. Unlike the mysteries of the faith, the reasons of her claim are cognisable by human reason; and this proclaims them indefeasible. It is true that her divine right to "teach all nations" has reference to spiritual truth only; but this embraces of necessity the right to exclude from the Catholic school everything different from or contrary to the faith of which she is the depository, guardian, and expounder. Every baptised Christian is in her charge. For every soul on which the Christian character has been impressed she has to answer before God; and never can she, without direst necessity, permit an influence other than, or hostile to, her own to warp or colour the young souls given to her charge.

How, then, it may be asked, do we see everywhere non-Catholic influences allowed to enter the Catholic school, and Catholic ecclesiastics engaged in making transactions of this kind? The answer is—it is one thing to lay down Catholic principles, another to reduce them to practice. The Church is bound by her duty as teacher to declare the truth fully, clearly, inexorably. On the other hand, in dealing with the secular power she is constantly engaged in making terms—giving away some portion of her right—either because she cannot help it, some Bismarck of the day compelling her by brute force; or to gain some advantage she thinks worthy of the sacrifice.

We distinguish in the Church, and especially in the Pope, two duties, two powers. One, to teach the Catholic faith in the clearest and fullest manner; the other, to administer Catholic affairs. As teacher, the Pope acts dogmatically and inflexibly; as administrator, he acts diplomatically, conditioning that the compromise never extends to any first principle of the faith, nor to any violation of the moral law. For example, the Pope elected to allow England to fall into schism rather than permit Henry to repudiate his lawful wife. It is well known that Pius the Ninth incurred the active hatred of the Jews, and preferred to brave the calamities thus brought on him rather than surrender the child Mortara, although only baptised clandestinely, to be taught to blaspheme his Saviour. To preserve the natural right of the Jewish parent, the Popes made a law forbidding Jews to employ Christian servants. When the Mortara family violated this law, and the Christian servant baptised the child, the Pope was bound to enforce the higher right of our Lord to that soul, although his throne was endangered by it. These examples show sufficiently the inflexibility of the Holy See when it is a question of first principles in faith or morals. Speaking broadly, it is not open to us to question the wisdom of the Holy See in making concordats with Cæsar. In these the Pope acts as chief ruler of the Church, and as guardian of the moral law. His decisions are, therefore, irreformable, and in any case they are taken on facts and motives, mostly outside the cognisance of the world. Moreover, these great acts are done with exhaustive care and deliberation, and are marked with certain forms which assure their authenticity and authority.* Very different is such action to that of the majority of the Irish hierarchy in consenting to the fatal compromise in Catholic education. This we are free to denounce as a betrayal of their highest trust, not only because the National system has a non-Catholic (that is, in this connection, an anti-Catholic) principle for its foundation, but because the compromise was unnecessary, and therefore unjustifiable.

In this matter of education there are, speaking broadly, four interests—four rights—namely: the Church's right, the child's right, the parent's right, the national right. One of these, his own, may for the moment be held to be within the bishop's province to make void. But what earthly right had he, without commission or delegation, to make away with the other three? It is impossible just yet to come at any certain record of the negotiations between Dr. Murray and Sir Thomas Wise which resulted in the foundation of the so-called National System; all that is certain on the matter is that Dr. Murray held no proxy for the Irish Church, and certainly Sir Thomas did not represent the Irish people.

Was the Castle bishop justified in consenting to it, and forcing it on his brother prelates, who were wiser than he? .It seems to me he was not. He was clothed with certain great trusts. Their guardianship was an intimate, essential portion of his duty. They had regard to the highest interests of his people. Surely he should not have been their

---

* This definition will show that the late unhappy Propaganda Circular cannot be included in the category of authentic or authoritative Papal pronouncements.

betrayer? The establishment of a system of Irish Catholic education was the corollary and complement of Emancipation. The battle had been fought and won. The victory meant the full equality of Catholics before the law. There was only necessary to complete it some courage, some consistency, some patriotism, some Catholic spirit. The Castle bishop was wanting in these qualities, and he weakly and ignominiously yielded—nay, forced on the Holy See compliance with a proposition false in principle and impossible in practice. I am not insensible to the valuable results of the National system; but they have come, not because of but in violation of its first principle—because the majority of the schools are denominational and not mixed. It must be said, too, that the system owes its partial success to the fact that it has had, especially of late, in its administration, several highly accomplished and very able men—the only examples, it may be said, in the whole range of the Irish executive, of men who loyally and faithfully served the Government, and preserved unstained and undimmed their faith and character as Catholics and Irishmen.

Still, the system could not evade the law of its being, nor escape the multiplied defects and perversions to which its constitution laid it open. These are familiar to all who have made a study of educational matters, and to the general public are partially known by the indiscreet revelations of Miss Whateley. To demonstrate how far it is from being a satisfactory provision for our educational needs, I will now proceed to define the nature and scope of Catholic education.

Education, in the broadest sense, is the development of the pupil—physically, intellectually, and morally—to the highest perfection of which his nature is capable. To reach this ideal, the operations should be coincident; for if you develop the physical nature of man to the neglect of the others, you make a powerful brute; if his intellectual to the neglect of the moral, a clever devil; if his moral to the neglect of the other two, a pious fool; if altogether in the way most suited to the subject, you gain the great end—"a sound mind in a healthy body" and make a good citizen and a good man. To use the words of a great authority, you attain the result "which enables a man to fulfil justly, skilfully, and magnanimously all the offices, public and private, of peace and war."

In a more restricted sense, education has for object the formation of the judgment and the direction of the will—the teaching of the child to discern and love what should be loved and to hate what should be hated. What does a sensible parent most desire to find in the child just finished school life? Surely, such knowledge and accomplishments as become his or her station in life and future occupation; but far beyond and above these, a judgment quick to sift truth from falsehood, clear in analysis, sagacious and broad in view; and before even this, a will strongly and firmly bent towards everything right and good.

Education is essentially a spiritual matter. As man's soul is his noblest part, what concerns it must take precedence of all else. Now, we cannot communicate with non-Catholics in spiritual things; and the Castle bishop, in consenting to the mixed system, violated a clear principle of Catholic theology. "All knowledge is one, springing from the eternal unity of God," says Cardinal Manning. Its communication, therefore, must be one, as the pupil is one. It is a unique work, beginning at the mother's knee, continued in the primary and intermediate schools, and finishing at the university. To be a complete it must be a harmonious work, springing from one root, and developing logically through all its stages. No part of it can contradict or thwart the other without producing confusion, and failing in its chief object. The mere statement of those principles makes an end of the "mixed" system. It is impossible to regard it, with its detestable jargon of "time-table" and "conscience clause," without indignation, for it conceals the denial of the first right of a people to a school which represents their religion and history; it is the mutilation of the intellectual life of the nation, and the endeavour to deprive it of its true and natural development. It would be just as easy to separate the child's soul and body and unite them again as to provide that at a certain moment the religious element shall enter or be excluded from the school. It is in effect an attempt to shut out the Almighty for a time from his rightful domain, and to admit his enemy thereto.

AN IRISH CATHOLIC LAYMAN.

THE CASTLE BISHOP AS EDUCATOR.

SIR,—I repeat—knowledge is one, the pupil is one, the school which deals with them should likewise be one. One in idea, one in operation, beginning with the greatest of professions: "*Credo in unum Deum,*" and developing from that root harmoniously to the end. This work, moreover, of Catholic education is mainly spiritual, and essentially positive and objective. It is the superimposition of the supernatural on the natural; or, rather, the informing of the latter by the former as intimately as the soul of man informs his body. Compromise, therefore, and negation are abhorrent to its principles and fatal to its results. They mar its completeness and perfection, no matter how slightly they intervene in its working. If for only the shortest space the "mixed" principle is introduced into a Catholic school, it destroys its character, since it is an admission of the condemned principle that the name or idea of God can or ought to be excluded from the work of education. It is in little, and for the time being, precisely the same theory as is written large in the model school and Godless college. All these ingenious contrivances which we see in convent schools for displaying the Holy Rood and other religious emblems, and putting them out of sight, at certain hours, or in presence of the inspector, are so many practical denials of the faith, though nothing may be farther from the intention of those using them. And these things are done in schools not one pupil of which is non-Catholic.

But it is only when we raise our eyes to the highest end of Catholic education that we perceive how indefensible and even detestable is everything hostile to its principles. This chief end is the carrying on in the intellect the work begun by the Church in the Christian soul. It is the expansion in the world of the Christian idea and making it prevail, not in the conscience of the individual only, but in the family, in society, in business, in science, in politics, in legislation, in government, in every concern of life, nay, even in the battle-field, when deadliest passions rage : when the priest fulfils his Godlike task amidst the iron hail, and the Sister of Charity with calm heroism offers her life to aid the dying. The Christian idea! What mind that has ever truly seized it can contemplate it without emotion?—that wonderful thought, the barest suggestion of which moves the faithful heart and suffuses the eye with the dew of love ; the beginning and end of all things ; the sweet savour which preserves and sanctifies human society, and opens to man the possibility of regaining the Eden he had lost. The Christian idea! The perpetual dwelling of Jesus Christ in the world He has created amidst the people He has redeemed. The assertion of His supreme and sovereign rights in the conscience and intellect of man, and of His power in the external order—exercised through His Church and bounded only by the limits He has Himself set—in the freedom of the human will. It is the displacing this grand central thought from its pre-eminence which makes the modern world sick nigh to death, and scuds our boasted civilisation staggering blindly, viciously, brutally back to paganism. Sad necessity it is which obliges the re-statement of what should be in the minds of all from the dawning intelligence of youth to the extremity of age, but which the world, and those who go with it, seek to forget or put out of sight.

The fulness of time had come ; the miracle of miracles was to be wrought ; the one transcendent fact of human experience was to occur.

All creation stood expectant—waiting that which was to radically modify its relations with its Creator. It came, and became for us the law of our life, the light of our intellect, and the means of our salvation. This fact is the Incarnation. Two thousand years has not dimmed the glory of its brightness nor lessened its value by the shadow of a shade. It stands amidst the centuries of man's history alone and unapproachable. To it all antiquity looked forward; and if posterity regard it with less eager and yearning gaze, it is because for us it remains living and energising in our midst. It is still, as of old, set for the fall and the resurrection of men. Those who are called to know it in its fulness it transforms and raises to the practice of heroic virtue. The multitudes to whom, in all their wanderings it is an object of deepest reverence and humble hope it saves. Those to whom it is a hard saying, who will not receive it, who turn away and walk with their Saviour no more—those who reject it, or scoff, or mock—it is not for them a source of life but of death. Human reason itself declares the absolute, all-embracing, all-absorbing, nature of this ineffable event. As God is the Sovereign Good, the sole self-subsisting, infinite, eternal Being, it necessarily follows that all things must begin and end in Him. Everything relating directly to Him or to His manifestation to His creatures must, in the Eternal Mind, take precedence of all other motives. The whole scheme of creation, therefore, must have been framed in relation to the Incarnation; nor, as far as human prescience can discern, would anything of which we have cognisance been created save to serve as a preparation and a shrine for this stupendous mystery.[*] Again, I repeat, this fact is not dead, nor merely historical, but living, energising, vivifying: the first cause and principle of all created things. It can neither be put aside nor let alone. It would be more possible and more wise to shut out the sun from the material universe than to close the moral order, or, indeed, the sum of human existence, against it—to extrude the Saviour of Men from the world He has redeemed. To imprint in ineffaceable characters the knowledge of Jesus Christ on the youthful mind is the noblest office of the Christian school, as it is that of the Church to make his love prevail in the heart. They are indissolubly associated in this glorious work, and to divide them is to strike as deadly a blow at Christianity as would be the sundering of the man and woman whom the sacred bond of Christian marriage had made one.

---

[*] A learned friend points out that I have here stated the Scotist theory, which though permitted, is opposed by the Thomists. Whichever be theologically strongest, it would seem that the former is most conformable to human reason, and certainly most attractive.

This event altered the whole relations of human society with its Creator. Whatever of right or authority the natural order possessed vanished in presence of Jesus Christ, reigning in and through the society He founded. No longer Creator only, He became our Redeemer, and more, our Brother and Lover and Friend. So infinitely attractive is this thought, so irresistibly does it appeal to everything that is best in man— to his reason as well as to his heart—that the Apostle pronounces anathema on those who close their understandings or harden their hearts against it. "If anyone love not the Lord Jesus let him be accursed." Henceforth mankind is segregated into two classes: those who know and receive this Divine fact, with all it implies, and those who know it not, or, still worse, reject it. Between these two an unfathomable gulf is fixed, to be bridged over indeed by God's grace for those who respond to its inspirations, to remain impassable to all who lift themselves above the humility of the Gospel. Of the former the Catholic bishop is the chief. It is his highest duty to guard and magnify this first of principles and make it prevail, and this the Castle bishop fails to do, because he has compromised his independence.

In this mystery of mysteries is the sum of human knowledge. It reaches from end to end, and enables us, as far as our present condition permits, "to know even as we are known." The ascetic spirit, the love of the Cross, the desire of self-sacrifice born of it, is necessary to the well-being—in the long run, to the very existence—of human society in any state above the savage. The office of the Catholic bishop is to guard and teach the truths of the faith; his chief duty is to render these from the abstract to the concrete, to reform and build up human society on the Christian basis, to make the Christian idea the informing and dominating principle of life. In this creative and Godlike office his chief external instrument is the school. In consenting to its degradation the Castle bishop has cut off his own right hand. It is not because of, but in despite of, the late Archbishop Murray, and his following in the Episcopacy, that the "mixed" system is not dominant in Ireland, with the Godless Queen's University for its apex, spreading on all sides intellectual confusion and moral corruption.

The first right of a people is to live; the second to fulfil the end of their existence by serving God in the way He has commanded, and by developing their national life on the lines of its genius. Both these rights have been denied the Irish nation until their concession could be no longer withheld. With the connivance and co-operation of the Castle bishop the latter has been granted in such mutilated form as to rob it of half its value. I claim as a primary right, a right both natural and supernatural, the presentation by my religious guides of the Christian idea in

F

its fullest and most objective form.   I claim from those whose duty it
is to teach and defend it that they shall make it operative throughout, and most of all in the school; · that they shall see that it pervades
and dominates the whole work of education, in books, statues,
pictures, music, pious ejaculation—in everything by which the all-
important work of education can be coloured and directed.   This is the
claim we, as Christians, have a clear right to make.   This is the claim
the Castle bishop practically denies.   He says, in effect, you are well
enough off with a crumb in place of the loaf which should be yours.
Knowledge deprived of its best quality is good enough for you.
There is something most cruel as well as unjust in this denial.   Ireland has
given everything the world holds valuable to retain intact the Christian
faith ; and a portion of her hierarchy so act as to deprive her of a great share
of the fruits of her sacrifice.   It is a mystery not to be solved by human
intelligence—how this nation, faithful above all, has been abandoned by
some of its spiritual chiefs to the grievous prolongation of its suffering.
Like Him whom she has enshrined in her heart of hearts, Ireland struggles
towards her salvation by the way of the cross.   The object of the scorn
and hatred of the world, reviled and mocked by her enemies, abandoned
and betrayed by her friends, buffeted and scourged by tyrants, she falls,
but she rises again, and goes on her painful way to the victory now,
thank God ! all but assured.   Weak and spent to the worldly eye, she is
strong by the Divine power which dwells within her, and by that she
will assuredly triumph over her enemies, and enter on the full enjoyment
of her rights.   If Christianity be true, the Christian order of society
should by right obtain.   Let its guardians begin by making it dominate
in the school.   If Christ reigns there He will soon reign in the external
order ; and we will have again in the island, once of saints, a reproduction
of its earlier glories.

I am, sir, yours, &c.,

AN IRISH CATHOLIC LAYMAN.

P.S.—It being undesirable to interrupt the sequence of the letters,
I will ask you to find room in a postscript for a further word to the
" I. C. Clergyman."   He does not believe in a Castle bishop.   How, then,
will he characterise the Cardinal's denunciations of the Land Leagues,
and his praises of the Forster *regime ?*   What will he call the Bishop of
Elphin's support of The O'Conor Don, after the latter had been sworn of
the Privy Council (to assist in imprisoning far better men than himself)
and had joined the Orange Emergency Club in Kildare Street?   What
will he call the action of a prelate playing detective on his own priests
in the Castle interest ? or that of the one who presented a most estimable

priest with a Forster *lettre de cachet* in one hand, and in the other a suspension, to force him to commit political suicide? If the "I. C. C." is as innocent as he seems to be of knowledge of this kind, I can give him in private, if he wishes, further examples proving beyond doubt that there are "Castle bishops," and that they do now and again things that in less exalted persons would be called by very ugly names.

The "I. C. C." is delighted that I should record my humble admiration of the Bishop of Achonry. I was proud of the opportunity, and would be glad to offer an equal homage to the patriotic and benign prelate who rules Killala with truly paternal spirit, regretting that the well-known patriotism of both is not permitted freer play. But, then, the "I. C. C." proceeds to make me answerable for something said by an unnamed American paper of a most objectionable nature, and in exactly the opposite sense of what I said!

The "I. C. C." having lived in Ireland for the last three years, insinuates a defence of "law and order!" Would it not be well for him to remember that in the mouths of those who use the phrase it means the violation of law and the provocation of disorder?

It is when he deals with the duty of obedience that he seems to forget the first principles of government and social order. There is no analogy between the time in which St. Paul wrote and ours. That was of the Pagan order, this of the Christian. St. Paul did not mean that we should be subject to any authority but to a rightful authority. He did not mean that we should obey every command, but only lawful commands. For instance, if the "firm and gentle" Spencer proclaimed that every Papist in Ireland should eat beef on Fridays, I presume the "I. C. C." would not hold we were bound to obey. Neither, probably, does he hold that because St. Paul sent back the slave to his master he thereby meant to uphold or defend the assertion of property in human beings. St. Paul himself was no serf. He withstood the unjust judge, and stood on his rights as a Roman citizen.

Finally let me assure the "I. C. C." that Catholicism is not a religion of slavery, but of freedom. We are free through the truth; we are free with the freedom by which Christ makes free. We are free interiorly because we know our duties and are willing to fulfil them; our rights, and are determined to maintain them. We are free because we are inspired by our faith with the love of freedom, and with the courage and self-sacrifice necessary to win and defend it. It was a Catholic archbishop who wrung the great charter of English freedom from a tyrannical prince. It was St. Thomas à Becket—the grandest figure in English history—who worsted, with the sacrifice of his life, one much more dangerous, and retarded the reformation by four centuries. St.

Laurence O'Tool also gave his life for the freedom of his nation. In about half a century Ireland will begin to understand how much of its newly-conquered liberty it owes to the noble, magnanimous independence of spirit of John McHale, Archbishop of Tuam. If the "I. C. C." will go back on his earlier studies he will find all the conditions laid down which not only justify but require resistance to authority when it has violated the law of its own existence.

P.S. 2.—Since writing the foregoing, a fact worth recording has reached me. In a southern town a spacious convent school was built some years ago. A large cross in bas relief adorned its front. The National Board Inspector refused to certify the school until this was removed; and the parochus *had it covered over.* This act of quasi apostasy, in the midst of a purely Catholic people, still remains an outrage and a danger to the faith.

THE CASTLE BISHOP AS EDUCATOR.

Sir,—To many it may seem a wearisome and useless iteration to insist on the claim of the Irish people to Irish and Catholic education; yet when it is remembered that we have half a century of wrong-doing to overcome, and many false principles ingrained in our present condition to expose, no pains will appear too great.

The natural, even in the most Christian society, resists the supernatural. Man craves his original freedom, though by the fall he lost the faculty of using it reasonably. Nature resists grace, and dislikes, when it does not hate, the cross. Not only inclination and passion, but all the power of the senses, the daily habit of life, tend to make the ascetic spirit as difficult of retention as of creation. The most important part, therefore, of the work of the Christian school is that of moral discipline, in filling the minds of its pupils with a sense of the value and nobility of sacrifice as the root of everything meritorious in the individual or valuable in society.

If this be a necessary part of the work of the school where the Christian idea dominates, how incomparably more so must it be in a society where it struggles for existence? Now, the Castle bishop, by destroying the unity of the Christian school (by the admission of the "mixed" principle), has made its highest work impossible. The true order and sequence of ideas—the union of reason and conscience, the harmony of the intellect and will—above all, the constant, abiding sense of the unseen and the supernatural—of the one thing necessary—these are never to be found in schools tainted by the "mixed" or "secular" principle, and but rarely, and in slender form, in those into which the State or secular authority enters as the director of studies or distributor of rewards. The constant tendency of every Government, whether it consist of one man or of many, is towards extending its own power at the cost of the liberty of its subjects—that is to say, all Governments naturally move towards despotism. The State being of right supreme in the natural order, but not having the faculty or power of defining its bounds, constantly strays beyond them, and seeks to make the spiritual power subservient to its own ends. In this country we know too well how despotic a practically-irresponsible bureaucracy may become. The natural counterpoise of this evil is to be found only in the Christian school, and, therefore, it is a misfortune for society when the State interferes with its management or leavens its spirit with its own. The robust and manly Catholic spirit which hates oppression, and resists it by every lawful means ; the exact knowledge of one's own rights, and respect for those of others ; these are only to be found where the Christian idea raises and tempers the natural man, and teaches him to live for other interests than those of time or sense. I re-assert, then, for every soul on which the baptismal waters have conferred the Christian character, the first of all rights, that of having the Christian idea presented to it in all its beauty and holiness, in all its fulness and power. I claim that the Christian character shall be as strongly impressed on the intellect by the school as it is on the soul by the Church. And if this first of rights be common to all who profess the Christian faith, how much more is it the due of that nation which has sacrificed all for its sake ?

The supremacy and absolute and universal nature of the Christian idea being set forth, let us now see how the Castle bishop dealt with it. Having consented to its obscuration in the National school, he went on to consent to its obliteration in the Model school, Godless College, and Queen's University. In this basest of betrayals of the highest interests of his people he was foiled mainly by Frederick Lucas and Dr. McHale, while Pius the Ninth made further advance on his downward course impossible. No doubt there will be urged in his favour his good intentions. Well, in this connection they are clearly of the order with which a certain place is paved. It seems to me also that in matters of this kind no one has a right to think wrongly. Opinion, surely, is not free as to whether or not a Christian people shall or shall not have Christian schools. Opinion is not free as to the right of the existence or non-existence of one of the three bases on which the Church raises the structure of Christian civilisation. If we look across the Channel we see the Cardinal of Westminster fighting the battle of the Christian school, with all the wealth and resource of a splendid intellect, against odds which would bring despair to the heart of any but a genius and a saint,

while here the Castle bishop, without a struggle, abandons the key of
the position and aids the enemy in effecting a lodgment from which it
will be difficult to expel him.

In the struggle between the Church and the world the Castle bishop
has tied his right hand behind his back.   In the reconstitution of the
Irish nation he has spoiled—he could not entirely destroy—one of the
main elements of the work.   A great genius might possibly estimate all
the evils to which his errors have given rise—God alone knows all the
good he has prevented.   The schools of Ireland would probably by this
time have become as renowned as they were in the centuries when
Europe flocked to Bangor and Lismore and Armagh, to learn of Irish
saints and doctors the wisdom not only of this world but of the next.
The success, even in the intellectual order, of the Irish Christian schools
would, if fully known, furnish the strongest argument against the
extension through the empire, and even abroad, of the agnostic principle
in education, and turn the tide now so strongly setting in this ruinous
direction.

It may be said that all this is matter of the past—that whatever
mistakes have been made have been condoned, and no good end can be
regained by reviving their memory   Did the Castle bishop show any
sign of repentance and amendment   Ireland would hail the return with
joy and remember the danger and injury no more.   But this is precisely
what he does not do.   The present condition of education in Ireland—
scandalous in every sense—is a proof that he still breaks the unity of the
Irish Church and paralyses its action in this all-important particular.
We have an equally strong proof in the dealing of some of the bishops
with the Order of the Christian Brothers, that the old "stoneblind"
policy is as active and as dangerous as ever.   Repeated attempts on the
integrity of the order have been made.   Perhaps in the whole range of
attempted confiscations none more extraordinary has been seen than in
that resolution of the Synod of Maynooth which calmly passed over all
the property of the order to the bishops.   Barring the difference of
intention, it was as flagrant an invasion of rightful ownership as any
carried by the eighth Henry, or the later robberies of France or Sardinia.
We do not forget the expulsion from Mallow ; and one Catholic prelate
has quite recently declared that the attack on the order will be renewed
on the first opportunity.

Yet the work of this self-sacrificing and most meritorious body is the
only part of our educational system on which we can dwell with satisfaction.   The writer has it on the authority of Sir John Lentaigne, the
highest probably which can be quoted in this connection, that the work
done at Artane is unrivalled throughout the world in extent and

excellence, while the fame of the Christian schools of Cork and Limerick has penetrated everywhere. As good work, in proportion, has been and is being done in their smaller schools. In the thoroughness of this work they illustrate some of the highest qualities of Catholic education, namely, truth of conception and logical coherence of ideas, continuity and harmonious development of intellectual life, and from these consistency of character and elevation of aim and purpose. Nor are the finer developments of educational science wanting. The play of fancy, the far-reaching knowledge, the keen analysis, the luminous view embracing all the qualities and accidents of a subject, the bringing together of "new things and old" to illustrate the present: these qualities and acquirements are far from being uncommon in those who have been fortunate enough to follow the Brothers' higher course. The publication of the intermediate lists shows how solid and general is the instruction they give, though the cramming of clever boys for passing in special subjects is certainly far below their high educational ideal. What is it in this noble body of men which excites the hostility of the Castle bishop? Really it is hard to say, except that they be too Irish and too Catholic. Having accepted a system antagonistic to the Christian, he cannot abide an Order which is for him a perpetual reproach, and in which not only the superiority of the theory but the highest results of Catholic education are most clearly seen. Surely it is nothing less than a manifest provision of Providence that amidst the general confusion a standard such as this should be preserved to form the foundation stone of the re-constructed edifice of Irish education.

I am, sir,

AN IRISH CATHOLIC LAYMAN.

THE CASTLE BISHOP AS EDUCATOR.

SIR,—In the emasculation of the Irish Catholic school two chief rights, two paramount interests, were sacrificed, namely, the right of the child to have the Christian idea stamped on his mind in ineffaceable characters, and the sovereign right of Jesus Christ to reign supreme in the intellects as well as in the souls He has redeemed.

So dangerous is it to palter with first principles, so difficult is it to retrace the first false step, to regain lost ground in the face of a powerful enemy, that the Irish Church has never since the first fatal compromise been able to take its rightful position or formulate a scheme for the settlement of Irish Catholic education. Having got off the king's high-way into a crooked and muddy bypath, our chiefs do not seem to have

the power to get back again.   The question is dealt with piecemeal—
now one part, now another, taken up.   Compromise follows compromise
until the confusion becomes worse confounded, and we are landed in a
muddle as scandalous as it is detrimental to the nation's intellectual
life.

One effect of all this is that the Irish mind has got into a state of
profound distrust of the members of the hierarchy who have had the
conduct of the matter.   If it be alleged that there has been guile and
deceit on the part of the Government, it is just as clear that there have
been on the Catholic side weakness, inconsistency, and vacillation.   The
negotiations have dragged on in an aimless, intermittent way, which
shows there was before the minds of those who had charge of the subject
no clear, intelligent purpose, no real knowledge of the wants of the
country, nor any firm determination to supply them.   Some provision
had been made for the instruction (one cannot call it education) of the
humbler sort.   To ordinary minds it would occur that the next thing
would be to provide suitable education for the middle class—that class
which has the same relation to society in general as the backbone has
to the human body, and which, being formed and strengthened properly,
keeps in health and order the classes above and below.   For this great
class—the backbone of the nation—no suitable provision has been made
nor attempted, nor apparently even so much as imagined.   Until this
was done, the long abortive struggle over the University would seem like
providing a roof for a building not yet raised above the foundations.
Yet, as certainly as that we can have no Christian order of society without
Christian education, we can have no middle class informed of its duties
and able to fulfil them without ample provision of middle-class schools.
This brings us to the distinction of the three, or rather four, classes into
which education is naturally divided.   First, the primary school.   For this
the three "R's," with some exercise of the reasoning faculty—some means
by which boys of special aptitude shall be enabled to go on to a higher
course—are sufficient.   More in our circumstances would be too much.
Awakening the fancy or cultivating the sensibilities of a man who has to
live in an Irish cabin, and earn scantiest subsistence by severest toil,
would be adding hardship to a lot already all but intolerable, and pre-
paring disturbance for the community.   For the child of the middle
classes, the large farmer, the thriving shopkeeper, the skilled tradesman,
the smaller manufacturer, a very different provision has to be made, for
on him the chief work of all civilised communities falls.   He has to take
up and develop all the arts of life.   He touches the labourer on one hand
and reaches the professional classes and even the aristocracy (though
this is neither necessary nor desirable) on the other.   The one class he

has to lead, the other to restrain. On him depends greatly the condition of the toiler, and, if he be a true man, he will keep from the excess and corruption, into which they are so prone to fall those who by an abuse of terms are called the "better classes." This catalogue of duties, which might be enlarged, shows how essential to the welfare of society is the proper training of the middle-class, and how destructive of all progress must be its absence. The root and primary cause of all our trouble is in the fact that we are not allowed to provide for our own wants in our own way. But all the secondary causes which have led to the decay of society in Ireland do not equal in evil effect the want of the middle-class schools. It cannot be said that our system of middle-class education is defective or insufficient ; it does not exist at all. We have the primary school for the labourer, the colleges (too many perhaps) for the professional man, and nothing between. Now, it may be seen at a glance that neither the primary school nor the college is fitted for the work to be done. To put a middle-class lad into a National school is like putting a watchmaker into a forge to learn his art. To put him into a college is to waste his best years and unfit him for business. Neither of these schools can by any possibility give what is wanted, neither can properly train him for his place in life.

For this there is needed what may be called, for want of a better name, a thorough grammar school education—a full knowledge of English, and a fair acquaintance with one other language—French, for choice. I hope that day may come when Irish will be added, since no one can properly understand the country in its nomenclature or history without knowing the language. Add to these mathematics, a knowledge of the elements of logic, or the art of thinking in a straight line and avoiding irrelevancy, and as much science as will enable the boy to understand and take an interest in the material world around him. Above all, I would insist on a full knowledge of the philosophy of history, which will open for him the book of human life; and the philosophy of religion, which will bind in one all his other knowledge, and give him a clear view of God's dealings with his creatures, and his own highest duty. There is nothing impossible or redundant in this curriculum ; and if it have the further conditions of being imparted at the boy's own door, or while he is under his father's roof, growing up in the atmosphere of the family and the business, and that it shall be at such a price as will not be beyond a moderate income, we have all necessary elements of a sound middle-class education. In the total absence of any such provision, what do we see ? The youth of the country growing up in want of almost all the instruments of thought and means of advancement, or sent to schools quite unsuited to their wants.

A well-to-do trader has a son to whom he wishes to give an education superior to what he had a chance of getting himself. He looks around and finds the only place open is the college. At a cost often too great for his means he places his boy in one of these institutions, excellent, it may be, in its way for its own purpose. The boy grinds away at classics for three or six years. His father, innocent man, imagines he will repay the cost, and be a help to him in his business affairs; but, when "finished," he discovers too late that his money is worse than wasted for the purpose he had in view. The lad, most likely, can't write a decent letter, nor do a simple sum in figures. But, far worse than these deficiencies, he has acquired what is unfortunately so common in Ireland, a vulgar, snobbish contempt for honest labour. Probably he is ashamed of the shop, possibly of his humble parents. He wants to be a lawyer, or a doctor, or a walking gentleman, professions all over-stocked in Ireland. The father goes over to the majority, the business falls into strange hands, its continuity and development are lost; often the trade leaves the town, and imported rubbish takes the place of sound home manufacture. Nothing is more palpable throughout the country than the decay of all the trades, and the importation of the commonest necessaries of life. For example, there are many important towns in Ireland dependent on London for household furniture, for no young man, whose father could give him the few thousand pounds necessary, will condescend to become a cabinet maker. The depletion begun by the withdrawal of taxes, carried on by absentee rents and interest charges, is tenfold aggravated by the business competition which this country is utterly unable to withstand, and so day by day we decline to extinction as a civilised, prosperous community, and every interest of life perishes from poverty and ignorance.

Supposing that to-morrow we were re-invested in our inalienable rights, no progress would be possible without the foundation of middle-class schools. This first necessary provision for the beginning of a better order has one formidable obstacle in its way, namely, the quiescence of the only persons able to take the initiative. No one can found a Catholic proprietary school without the sanction of the Ordinary,* and this is not so easily obtained as might be supposed. But, supposing that a sufficient number of qualified persons could be found to-morrow to place a school in every suitable locality, the difficulty would be nearly as great as ever; for no really good middle school can be carried on without the assistance of competent masters, and no one

---

* In a considerable town in the south of Ireland a wealthy proprietor offered to build, equip, and endow a middle-class school, and failed to get the sanction of the Ordinary. The reason given was that it might interfere with a diocesan college twenty-four miles distant !

with sufficient capital will invest it in schools and wait perhaps for years for the result. The most feasible plan, perhaps, would be the formation of an educational union analogous to the English Poor School Committee, but having the promotion of middle-class education for object. Now, it may be strongly asserted that the principal difficulty in founding middle schools is with the ecclesiastical chief in the various localities. In no considerable town will the incumbent have any great trouble in raising funds for a foundation, which must be provided if the school is to be permanent. Why he does not do so is a mystery no one can explain but himself. The want is there; the people are only too willing to provide for it; the way to do so is not opened to them. This requires no Government charter, no external aid. All that is needed is organisation, and abundant means of support will be at once forthcoming. To give a single illustration. Some years ago the bishop of a midland diocese visited a town within its borders. It was of considerable size, with a large district around, and the only educational facilities were two National schools of average merit. The bishop expressed himself very emphatically on the inadequacy of this provision, and declared that a middle school should be at once established. He looked round the town, and, finding a house of regular priests rather larger than needed for the community, he directed them to open at once a grammar school. It did not lie in the good fathers' way, it did not fall in with their ordinary work, but in obedience they complied. The school was opened, and over sixty pupils, paying full middle-class fees, at once attended. But the provision for their instruction was wholly inadequate. The school struggled on for two years, and, the pupils having fallen to one-third of the opening number, the school was closed.*

Two things are specially noticeable here. First, the demand. The pupils would have been doubled in a year if the school were what was wanted. Next, the bishop contented himself with directing what was to be done, and never took the least trouble about the means or the result. In point of fact, he never inquired about nor put his foot within the school from the day of its opening till its close. In this he followed the example of the Maynooth meetings before referred to. A discussion is held, resolutions are adopted, great promises are made, and expectations excited. Then the bishops retire to their own districts, and nothing is done. It is perfectly obvious that had the hierarchy resolved on a definite course on the education question—worthy of themselves, of the subject, and of the people they represented—they could have at any time for the last fifty years combined the Irish popular representation

---

* Several of the pupils of this middle school have since gone to one of Erasmus Smith's foundations, in defiance of the ecclesiastical authorities.

on this point, and forced from the English Government full satisfaction of their demands. The bishops are in the position of people who loudly assert their wish that a certain thing should be done, while, having it in their power, they don't take a single step towards the doing of it. In this relation many of them hold a position so inconsistent that it would become their dignity and authority to quit it as quickly as possible. They permitted in the National school the introduction of the secular system. The model school is only an amplification of that system. It provides, in almost every case, an excellent course of instruction for middle-class boys. But these schools are almost exclusively maintained for the benefit of non-Catholics, since they are prohibited to Catholic children. Discussing the disability with a distinguished official of the Education Board some time since, he said: "I do not challenge the right of the bishops to bar these schools to Catholic children; but I do assert that, having done so, they were bound to provide, or stimulate others to provide, a proper substitute." To this position there seems no sufficient answer.

Nothing can be more disadvantageous, nothing more trying to the loyalty and obedience of those who suffer, than the disability thus imposed. In a great northern town lives a friend, a good Irishman and Catholic. Providence has blessed him with seven sons, the eldest not yet twelve years old. Of limited means and modest ideas, he destines them all for business. The educational facilities open to him in the Catholic order are a National school and a college. In the former his children would learn so much not included in the school course that to send them there is out of the question. The college is quite above his means, and, besides, does not provide the education required. At his very door is a model school, one of the masters of which is a Catholic, and which gives all that is needed in the way of secular instruction. This master—a man of excellent character (he goes to a neighbouring diocese to discharge his religious duties !)—daily assembles the Catholic children, who attend in large numbers despite the prohibition, for prayers and catechism. The school is in every way (save in the principle which underlies it) one which would suit my friend's needs excellently, that is, taking the general state of education into account. But he is threatened with a denial of the sacraments if he sends his sons to it. With the officer of the National Board he says : " When my bishop prohibits the use of the only school within my reach, why does he not—as he could do by only willing it—provide a proper substitute ? He has already admitted the mixed principle in the National school. The model school I want to use is practically the same, and if I use it I am outlawed. I must put up with such inferior home teaching as I can pay for, or send my boys to a school where they would be familiarised with manners of the rudest and ideas of the lowest kind ; and they will be handicapped in the struggle of life in such a way as to render success impossible."

Is this a position in which a man should be placed whose first desire is to do well his duty as a parent and a Catholic? The consideration of the answer must be reserved for the next letter.

I am, sir, your obedient servant,

An Irish Catholic Layman.

THE CASTLE BISHOP AS EDUCATOR.

Sir,—The case of my northern friend, saving that he has a burden rather heavier than common, is not singular. It exists wherever a model school is found, unless there be in the vicinity a middle-class school of the Christian Brothers. Over Ireland this instance may be multiplied by thousands, and the position gives rise to more heart-burning and alienation between the people and their spiritual chiefs than the latter seem to have an idea of. It is certainly a hard and cruel position for a man of good-will to find his duty as a parent and as a Catholic in direct antagonism. Now my friend's bishop is not "Castle" nor *faineant*. He is no monsignor who dwells apart and veils his dignity within the recesses of his palace. He lives with and for his subjects, and enjoys their affection and confidence as well as their veneration. He fills a position of the greatest difficulty with eminent ability and success. There is perhaps no bishop in Ireland who can show so much work thoroughly done in the same space of time.* But if such examples are found in the green wood what will take place in the dry? The almost universal and persistent neglect of the middle-class schools is giving rise to a general feeling of soreness and discontent which, unless the cause be removed, will add another potent element of disunion to the number already existing. To make the matter clearer, we must subject it to analysis, and endeavour to distinguish the relative rights and duties of the parties. The bishop has clearly the right to say to my friend, "I forbid you, under pain of deprivation, to send your children to the model school." But does the exercise of that right entail no duty? Can the bishop justly or wisely or rightly close one school-door without, if it be in his power, opening another? If my

---

* It may now, unhappily, be said that the bishop referred to was the late Dr. Dorrian. It may be also added that some provision for middle-class education has since been made in Belfast.

friend says, "I obey you, my lord, but I call upon you to lead the way in providing a proper substitute for the school you forbid—you will find me and all my class only too ready and willing to give the means," can the bishop decline the invitation without grave neglect of duty? The answer must be left to himself as supreme judge.

Let us now examine what are the rights and duties of the parent. In the natural order his authority in the education of his child is absolute, conditioning that it be not so used as to violate the moral law. This authority we have seen the Pope guarding when he was sovereign of the Roman States. The right of the bishop supervenes when the child is admitted into the Christian family. Now this admission does not do away with the original duty of the parent. It divides it indeed with the child's spiritual father; but on the other, the natural parent, the duty remains of fitting the child for his place in life. The duty and right of the one is in the physical and intellectual order; of the other, in the moral and spiritual. The right and duty of the natural parent as regards the child's physical and intellectual development remain entire. We will more clearly perceive its nature by an analogy. The laws both of nature and revelation oblige us to maintain the life of the body. To this end we take the best and most wholesome food. If this be not within our reach we take that which is not so good, yet fulfils its office, though less effectually. Wanting this, we take a quality still lower, till we come to that which is positively unwholesome and destructive of life. This we may not take, because by doing so we would become accomplices in our own death.

The parent is bound to provide for the child's intellectual nourishment. His obligation in this respect is not touched by the authority of the Church to provide for its moral training. For this he ought, if he can, place his child in a Catholic school, where knowledge, the mental pabulum, is supplied in its highest form—that is, illumined by the Spirit of Wisdom, and ordered and correllated by revelation. If this school, which I insist upon for the Catholic child as the clearest and most indefeasible of rights, be not available, he is bound to provide from non-Catholic sources such knowledge as is necessary for the child's future, with as little of naturalism or paganism as may be. And so on through many gradations till we reach the school which is destructive of faith and morals. This, it is clear, Catholics cannot frequent—no matter what mental destitution or social disability may result—no more than they may trample on the cross or offer incense to Jupiter to propitiate the rage of the heathen persecutor.

The analogy shows that the matter is one of degree and expediency, and of dual authority. The parent's duty, if it does not confer co-ordinate rights, surely entitles him to have a say in the matter. Is he ever consulted? Are his ideas and interests in his child ever taken into account? It would not appear so. He is treated as if non-existent, and decisions on these matters, not of principle—on these he has only to learn and submit—but of prudence and expediency, are come to without the least reference to him. In the northern town before mentioned non-Catholic boys have at their command half a dozen institutions excellently suited to give the needed training. Every day in a flourishing community opens new roads to advancement. The non-Catholic boy "keeps his powder dry," and waits upon occasion and opportunity. The Catholic does not guard the ammunition, because he never got it. He is hopelessly out of the fight, and the inferiority begot in evil times continues by reason of intellectual destitution.

It may be said, if the bishop just now in question be no "Castle" but a model bishop, how can the other be blamed in particular for what seems to be a general defect? Most justly he can, because it was his action led to it, and because his attitude makes an adequate settlement of the question impossible. He still prevents the preparation and presentation to our rulers of the Catholic educational claim ; and, even if it was formulated, he would still remain an obstacle, for he would not honestly join in the mandate to our representatives which alone could force the Government into compliance. When Mr. Parnell and the Irish members were forcing the passage of the Intermediate Act (a matter, by the way, on which the Catholic Whig and the Castle bishop preserve an absolute silence, if they do not claim the Act as their own) he found the greatest difficulty in bringing certain Irish members up to their duty. He was accused of calling them "Papist rats." Putting aside his own denial, the presumption is quite against the truth of the charge. He is too highly-bred a gentleman to use a term which would justly offend others beside the persons in question, and too prudent a general to give such an opening to the enemy. But if he called them by the most opprobrious epithet the language affords, would it express the measure of their degradation ? These same Catholic Whigs form as a class the best proof of the urgent need of the thorough reform of our educational system, especially in its higher grades.

This again brings us face to face with the question not now to be asked for the last time—Why has the Catholic University failed, and who is responsible for its failure ? Who shall answer to Ireland for the squandering of the enormous sum contributed for its foundation, and who for the still more lamentable waste of intellectual power, and the continued imposition of mental inferiority its fall involved ? Who can be properly charged with its career of inefficiency and its inglorious end ?

Not surely the grand and beautiful character whose fame gave *eclat* to its opening, and whose " University Lectures " remain the sole record of usefulness and honour connected with it.   Ireland will yet inquire why he was permitted to depart with as little recognition of his priceless services as if he were an incompetent usher ; for she is grateful not only for what was done, but for what might have been, and her honour is touched in this matter.

One answer only can be given.   The university was killed by the Castle bishop.   The need for it was of the greatest.   It was founded by the direction and had the fruitful blessing of the Holy See —that powerful blessing which has given life to every truly great educational centre throughout the world.   Yet these potent motors and the lavish generosity of the people could not prevail against West-British influence.   This was persistently and successfully bent on eliminating from the curriculum of this first of Irish schools everything distinctively Irish.   Provision was carefully made that nothing savouring of Irish feeling or Irish patriotism should be the outcome of its teaching.*   To this end all specially Irish studies were excluded, and the principal chairs filled by foreigners, some of whom had not the good sense or the good taste to conceal their anti-Irish spirit, or their contempt for the country whose sons they made a pretence of educating, and which gave them the bread they so badly earned.

Great as is the mischief the Castle bishop has done and is capable of doing, he will never surpass what he has achieved in destroying the Catholic University.   The Church can work miracles with the masses, but unless the leading intellects of a people run in national and Catholic lines her work is being continually undone.   When the thinkers of a nation—who are always less numerous than is commonly imagined—are not possessed with the Christian idea, what the Church builds up one day they throw down on the next.   They put the spiritual and intellectual orders in opposition, and when the former is not unusually active, the latter, being naturally in alliance with the worldly spirit, prevails. The result is a succession of catastrophes, of which the rebellion called the Reformation and the French revolution of '89 are the chief examples.

When, finally, the Catholic University, dissociated from the national life, came to perish of sheer inanition, and the country would no longer bear the annual collection for its support, a writer in an English Catholic paper pointed out the principal cause of its decay, and

---

* Special care seems to have been taken to guard against renewing the ancient traditions of Irish learning, connecting the past with the present, or doing anything which would go to build up a new Ireland in the national and intellectual sense.

quoted in support of his view some memorable words of the late Archbishop of Tuam. This letter caused quite a flutter in West-British Catholic circles, and indignant reclamations were made about its publication. The Dublin correspondent of the paper in question pronounced the quotation to be "scandalously false." Unfortunately for him, he had nothing to allege in support of his assertion, while the writer of the letter in question had abundant testimony to his accuracy from many persons who, like himself, were present and heard the words. With the usual "fairness" of English journals, the paper positively refused to insert argument or disproof of any kind, and the slanderer got off for the time.* The letter in question was thought worthy of notice by his Eminence of Dublin, who thus referred to it in a pastoral published shortly afterwards. The Cardinal sets out by declaring "the Catholic University is not dead, nor even does it sleep . . . . The University established by Papal authority to confer degrees in theology, scholastic philosophy, and canon law continues under the control of all the bishops of Ireland . . . . This University is a non-teaching institution. But under another aspect the Catholic University shall be a teaching body, and it shall be closely connected with the Royal University . . . Under this aspect it shall be entirely distinct from the Catholic University, and shall henceforth be distinguished as the 'Catholic University College.'"†

After reading this extraordinary series of contradictions, the first idea that occurs to one is to inquire, "What estimate does the Cardinal form of the intelligence of his readers?" First we have the unqualified assertion that the Catholic University, the great school which was to educate the highest mind of Ireland, was not only not dead, nor asleep,

* The writer referred to declared that he heard the late Archbishop of Tuam reply as follows to the address of the students of the Catholic University, on the occasion of the jubilee of his consecration : "Amongst all the addresses which I have received, this comes to me with peculiar pleasure and some surprise. For never since its beginning as a teaching institution have I aided your school by voice, or pen, or purse. You will naturally look for an explanation of such a statement, and I will frankly give it. When it was question of framing the curriculum of the university, after the chairs common to all universities—theology, philosophy, &c.—were founded, I thought that in an Irish Catholic school the special studies relating to Ireland should be provided for. I was withstood, and a spirit was manifested which I could neither work with nor accept. I took my hat, left the council chamber, and never returned." This report was pronounced "scandalously false," and all evidence of its substantial correctness (of which there is abundance) declined. The writer has since heard that when Dr. Mac Hale insisted on the necessity of establishing chairs for Irish history and literature, &c., &c., Cardinal Cullen asserted his supreme authority as Papal Delegate, thus ignoring not only the rights of the Irish laity, but of his own equals in the hierarchy.

† The title of "Catholic" has since been withdrawn by authority from "University College," as well as the library and everything else that could possibly help it in the work of education.

G

but living and acting. Next we have the detail of dissolution, and even dissection. The Catholic University as conferring degrees is to live in idea somewhere and somehow. The Catholic University as a teaching institution (to simple people the idea of a university apart from its teaching function is preposterous) is to exist no longer, but its duty is to be continued by a school called the Catholic University College, *'which, however, is to have no connection with the Catholic University, but to be affiliated to the Royal."* This, surely, must be the most wonderful school ever seen, which can be opposite things at the same time, and embody in its constitution contradictory ideas. We must look to the " stone-blind " West-British faction for this result.

An Irish Catholic Layman.

THE CASTLE BISHOP AS EDUCATOR.

Sir,—The Irish Catholic University died, and justly died, because it was dissociated from the national life. If the intentions of its managers had been reached, its product would have been a race of West-British Whigs—that is, of anti-Irish Irishmen. Better a thousand times it perished than continued that hateful class ; for torpid intellects are preferable to active when the latter are perverted. There is still, it is true, a " Catholic University College "* in Stephen's Green, but it is merely a college of the metropolitan See, in which a few professors of more or less excellence teach a few scholars in the halls of the whilom university. It is no more the school first founded in that locality than the decrepit son of a dead man is the man himself. It bears no resemblance to that seat of learning the light of whose science was to attract students from East and West, from far California and from the Antipodes, and be a centre of highest culture for every race of English speech. The prophecy has failed ; the promise was blighted ; the hope withered in the baleful miasma of Whiggery and West-Britonism which destroys when it touches everything Irish and Catholic. The utter failure of the university is apparent when one asks : " Where are the works of science and literature which it has produced ? Where the men of mark and cultivation, of 'light and leading,' who have issued from its halls, and illustrated its teaching? Where its influence on the mind of Ireland, in planting fruitful ideas, in ennobling public life ?" It was a weakling from its birth ; it has vanished, and left scarce a trace of its existence. Its failure will make the next attempt to found a university far more difficult ; but it will, at all events, warn the future founders not to repeat the errors of the past.

---

* Is it true that this college has six students and eight eminent professors ?

The history of the Catholic University will in due time be written. The materials are collected, and are, I understand, in competent hands. It will not be an edifying history; it will be one of warning. In the meantime it will be well to advert to one or two episodes in its life to point the present argument. What follows is written from memory, and, therefore, subject to correction ; yet I trust my recollection of the facts is sufficiently accurate to prevent material error. The university had gone far on its downward course, the annual collection was dwindling, the hope of success growing fainter, when certain members of the hier- archy approached the Government of Lord Derby with proposals for a charter and endowment. Partly, it may be, to "dish the Whigs," partly to settle a troublesome question, the Government entered into negotia- tions, which were carried (by the late Lord Mayo on the one side, and by, I think, Drs. Leahy and Moriarty (or Derry) on the other, to a considerable length. The charter of a purely Catholic University (with en- endowment) was conceded ; the question came to be the constitution of the senate and governing body. Under, we may well suppose, Whig Catholic inspiration, the bishops were induced to claim supreme and irresponsible power, to the exclusion of the lay element, even when this was to be the outcome of the university itself. That demand was put as an ultimatum. When this stage was reached the No-Popery faction in England began to move. The Government declined to accede to the demand, and retired from the negotiation. The bishops then got alarmed at the prospect of losing the only offer ever made by our rulers on any matter of education which respected Catholic principles. They offered to renew the negotiation on a more moderate basis ; but by this time the Government thought they had no more to gain than to lose by declining, and they are said to have replied to the altered demand of the bishops : " Her Majesty's Government never could have imagined that the Irish Catholic bishops could say what they did not mean," and there was an end.

Time passed on, and Mr. Gladstone essayed the settlement of the third Irish reform he had proposed. He appears to have submitted the University Bill in its general idea through Lord Emly to some of the bishops, and had it approved. The university he proposed being just an exaggerated Godless college, the Catholic spirit of the people, backed by the better judgment of the majority of the hierarchy, repudiated the Bill. The ministry was defeated ; Gladstone, indignant at what he must have thought a betrayal of confidence, retired and wrote " Vaticanism." It would look as if he blamed Lord Emly, for the latter has not appeared since in Government circles, and could get no better appointment for his son than that of principal domestic of a sham Court.

Some time after this fiasco, when it had become apparent to the world that the University was *in articulo mortis*, the writer meeting on the way to Dublin a bishop, a member of the Educational Committee, he ventured to urge strongly the reforming of the University. The bishop replied that the matter had already been finally arranged, and the institution given over bodily to the greatest society of teachers the world has ever known. Now the bishop spoke of a fact in which he was participant. He could not therefore be mistaken. Nevertheless, the transfer was not carried out,* and Dean Neville was charged with the revival of the all-but-defunct University. It is said this eminent divine left his pleasant quarters by the Lee with the notion that the Irish party would use their powers, which now began to be seen, though not acknowledged, to obtain the charter and endowment which were declined before. Whatever may be determined in the future, certain it is that the party would not speak one word nor move one motion to make the dean rector *magnificus*, with a munificent salary, of a revived school which, if it showed more intellectual activity, would assuredly be more tainted with Whiggery than before, and, finding his hopes were vain, he retired on the lines he had prudently left open.† It seems after that that the previous arrangement could not be resumed, and so this institution, once so bright with hope and promise, ended its useless and inglorious career. Under the guidance of the Castle bishop we have come down from the Irish Catholic University of 1851 to the Royal "University" of 1883. *Facilis descensus Averni.* How anyone, having regard to the meaning of words, could apply the noble and time-honoured title of "university" to this motley examining board passes comprehension. Not only is it not a university in the sense of teaching—it is not even one as examining. And its constitution! Catholic prelates, heads of Godless colleges, Episcopalians, Presbyterians, Unitarians, Nothingarians—and Thomas Maguire, impossible to class—all fitly presided over by the chief Freemason in Ireland—head of the impious sect which hates and wars against the Christian Name. How pleased and edified the Catholic members of the university must have been to see their Chancellor principal figure in the Orange orgies carried out in Belfast last week. Does the Irish Hierarchy know how this shameful compromise is regarded by the people? Was the Hierarchy justified in accepting it? I ask not as deciding, but seeking a decision. It would appear that in this the bishops, under whose supervision this nameless thing was

---

* It has since been effected with the result of raising the number of students, in a few weeks, from half a dozen to near one hundred.

† It is currently reported that the Dean was several weeks in Dublin in this year of grace (1887) exhausting the resources of diplomacy to gain access to the Castle by the back stairs.

produced, lost sight of their fiduciary character, and went beyond their rightful powers in leading the Irish people into this dismal swamp in which their faith as well as their nationality is imperilled.

This wretched sham is consistent throughout. A sum less than a third of what is given to the three Godless colleges is granted to all Ireland, non-Catholics as well as Catholics. Of this the professoriate takes a large portion, the administration and examiners a goodly part of the remainder, while the Senate swallows half the rest, and leaves £2,000 for the students! Again, these latter come from richly-endowed Trinity,* and even from Oxford and Cambridge, to snatch from the "Royal" students the miserable portion which should fall to them. When one passes the spacious portals of Trinity and thinks of the leisure and wealth and learning there devoted to the uses of a mere section of the population and to the maintenance of an unjust ascendency, it is impossible to repress a feeling of indignation at the cowardly and illegitimate compromises into which we have been led.

This paltering with Catholic principles in Education is, in the present condition of the mind of Europe, peculiarly unfortunate. Since the revolt of the sixteenth century, modern civilisation day by day widens the gulf between it and the power which brought it into existence. The Church had endued society with all the fruitful elements of civilisation, as Lecky acknowledges, and succeeded in Christianising the world "in the very hour that world became supreme." Then was pronounced anew the fatal "Non serviam," and society at once started on its retrograde course. Up to this time it has been held together in England partly by the Christian framework on which it was built up, partly by the illogical but highly practical common sense of the people, partly by their natural phlegm. All these, and the more indefinite but most real and invaluable public conscience which the Church creates in every community she civilises, are yielding to the dominant principle of English life. This is private judgment, which is in essence naturalism—that is, paganism. It is essentially a principle of disintegration, which, now slowly, now quickly, but always certainly, works through and destroys the cohesion of every community in which it takes root. Once a man is persuaded that he is his own prophet and priest he comes soon to the conclusion that he is his own sovereign, since the greater authority contains the less. English society is at length yielding to the universal solvent. It is being rapidly reduced to its primal elements of barbarism. Your English workman and labourer is a savage with a slight varnish of civilisation. Your educated Englishman is a pagan with the least (intellectual) tincture of Christianity. The change wrought by the last thirty years is significant. Then Atheism was apologetic and not "good style." Now it is audacious, and, when allied with science and a cultivated taste, rather held to be a distinction. The open profession of infidelity no longer debars a man from success in life, nor shuts to him any avenue of ambition. Meanwhile the paganising of every relation of life goes on— education, marriage, art, science, literature. Only by the intervention of the Irish party was the legislature recently saved from the intrusion of the most beastly form of agnosticism in the person of Mr. Bradlaugh— favoured, we profoundly regret to admit, by Mr. Gladstone, whose genius, if not principle, should have preserved him from this melancholy lapse.

Add to these active principles of dissolution the aggregation of vast masses of workers in the great manufacturing and mining centres living Godless and joyless lives, with passions brutalised and unchained, looking with covetous and jaundiced eyes on the luxury produced by their hopeless toil, and you have the elements (wanting only hunger to stir them into activity) of the most ferocious revolt the Christian era has seen.

As if to make this universal, modern Governments are every where engaged in banishing the very name of God from the schools. In one country of all modern states could the Christian idea be made to dominate, not only with the consent but in satisfaction of the ardent desire of the people, and in this they are deprived of this privilege of infinite value by the default of their spiritual chiefs. It cannot be repeated too often or too emphatically—till the change comes—that to the Castle bishop—to his want of courage, consistency, and principle— is owing the elimination of the Christian idea from the Irish educational system.

I ask again, who can tell what we lose, what the world loses, what the Church loses, by this thrice unhappy compromise? There are abundant evidences that the intellectual superiority of the Irish race remains; and we have many examples of the special aptitude of the Irish genius for the study and development of the queen of sciences. Perhaps before this time would have issued from a truly Irish Catholic University another Scotus to confute modern sophists and propound a philosophy which would compel the world of intellect back from paganism. The least issue of a thoroughly-organised system of Irish Catholic education would be the taking by Irishmen of the chief positions in their own country and in England, where now their place is mostly to be hewers of wood and drawers of water.

Let no one say in his haste this is extravagant. When we see Michael Davitt, with education gained haphazard, coming from a convict prison to inaugurate a revolution which has destroyed the strongest as it was the worst monopoly in the world, and speaking only yesterday to the most thoughtful portion of London society ; when we see Mr. Healy and Mr. Sexton, bred in the schools of the humble Christian Brothers, commanding the respectful attention of and forcing just legislation on the hostile senate of England, what may we not hope from an Irish educational system worthy of the people, and doing fullest justice to their intellectual powers ?

As long as the Castle bishop is left in his present place of influence, so long will everything Irish and Catholic perish under his hand. It is, then, a matter of simplest necessity for the Irish people to turn to their true leaders and guides—to the successors (and, thank God, they are many) of the late patriarch of the West, and ask these venerable prelates to embody in a Claim of Right the Irish Catholic educational demand. This is the first step ; the next is to instruct the representatives of Ireland to place this claim before the Imperial Parliament, and urge it in that persuasive manner they have of late become masters of. The land question is near a settlement, so that the way will be open for this most just demand, which can be urged *pari passu* with that still greater claim of the Irish nation to live its full and natural life within its own borders undisturbed and unimpeded by its hereditary enemies. In making their claim the bishops will have at their back the whole popular force, and we may rely on them that the terms they make will not be marred by the Whiggish element which has hitherto ruined every attempt at educational justice.

I am, sir, yours,

AN IRISH CATHOLIC LAYMAN.

P.S.—One word for " Albulfeda." I am sorry he thinks I have deteriorated. It is not consciously nor on the grounds he states. I never claimed educational monopoly for any class. I merely take facts as they are. Society is educationally divided into four classes—the man who works with his hands only, he who works with his head and hands, he who works with his head only, and he who is not bound to work at all. Here you have necessarily the divisions of primary, middle-class, professional, and what is properly called " liberal " education—or that which aims at the cultivation of the intellect for its own sake. If any of the humble ranks show exceptional ability I would not only permit them to go, but aid them on their journey to a higher place. This will not alter the fact that the bulk of mankind must always " earn their bread with the sweat of their brow "—a penalty the beneficence of which amply atones for its severity.

I. C. L.

THE CASTLE BISHOP AS EDUCATOR.

Sir,—The recent University celebrations constrain me again to ask the favour of your columns for a little while. The Royal University has had its annual meeting. Its Chancellor, having for his supporters two non-Catholics, went from the platform, when he beslavered his "Roman Cawtholic brethren" with hypocritical pretences of goodwill, to meet his real brethren in the Orange-Freemason Hall in Molesworth Street, where he was received with "tumultuous applause, largely mingled with Kentisn fire." There, no doubt, the murderous conspiracy against those same "Roman Cawtholics" was still further evolved, and Lord Ernest Hamilton sent down to Derry, as representative of his family, to incite the Orange mob to riot and outrage. The Cardinal spared us the shame of seeing him play second to this ignoble duke. He did not avoid the scandal of presiding at the Senate next day. Turn it round in any and every light, this same Senate is just the old Godless "Queen's" Senate under another name, with the addition of a few Catholic ecclesiastics. These do not in the slightest degree change the nature of the institution, nor entitle it one whit more to the confidence of the Irish people. From this position the question naturally arises, "Who or what does Cardinal McCabe represent in this false and dangerous compromise? Not the Irish Church, to which it is abhorrent. Note the scant attendance of Catholic ecclesiastics at the conferring of degrees. Not certainly the Irish people who were not consulted in its institution, whose interests it mocks, and who turn with indignation from its pretence of educational justice. The Cardinal represents simply and solely—himself.

We were assured lately, in solemn pastoral, that the Catholic University was not only not dead, but "living and active." It had abandoned, to be sure, its claim to confer degrees, but it was still a teaching institution "*affiliated* to the Royal University." Its last session opened with four students and eight professors. It was "too utter." The sham could be sustained no longer, and the University buildings (or more correctly, part of them) have been at length made over to those who will make good use of them.

Who is responsible for the squandering, with scarce any appreciable result of the vast sums (amounting in all, it is said, to £350,000) given out of their poverty by the Irish people for their chief school? These funds were a sacred trust. How were they disbursed? Was there an audit of any kind of the University accounts, or any check whatever on the expenditure? The Land League, with less than half the amount, made a revolution, one effect of which was to reduce the burthen on the

Irish tenantry from £2,000,000 to £3,000,000 a year. And the public were amply satisfied with the results. Yet an audit was called for most clamorously by those who never subscribed a shilling, and it was satisfactorily rendered. The managers of the Catholic University muddled away the enormous sum named in the attempt to found a school which should be Catholic and not Irish, with the result of passing over to their successors the University buildings swept of every thing but the dust of thirty years. It is open to grave question if the removal of the library was not as illegal as it was illiberal and unjust. It was a gift to the *locus* for teaching purposes; and whoever is answerable for having sent it to litter the floors of Clonliffe will yet have to answer to the Irish people. The Jesuit fathers may or may not be the proper persons for the place. That is not the question. They have been charged with the duty of carrying on the work of the Catholic University. They represent the interests of higher education in Ireland, and everything done to their detriment, every disability put upon them, every obstacle thrown in the way of their efficient working, every burthen, every penalty (and they have had all of these), is an injury to the highest interests of Ireland, for which an account will be demanded when the day of reckoning comes.

One of the first things to be done, when the reconstitution of Irish society comes to be undertaken, is to refound an university which shall be Irish as well as Catholic. And this of necessity if we mean to hold our own in the intellectual race, or take our place amongst the progressive peoples of civilisation. It may clear the ground for the attempt if we examine into the rights and duties involved. And, first, it is necessary to declare emphatically that it is not possible, in the present temper of the people, to propose the entrusting of any sum, large or small, for university purposes, to the hands which made such a fatuous use of the former fund. Nothing could be farther from my thoughts than to charge these with intentional malversation. However good the intentions of Cardinal Cullen and his associates, the fact remains that the money is gone and the university dead. From the constitution of the board of management it could hardly be otherwise. Ecclesiastics are almost invariably bad men of business. Their whole training is foreign to the conduct of affairs, especially when there is in question the judicious expenditure of money. It may be said that of the many millions spent in religious buildings in Ireland during the last fifty years one-fourth was worse than lost by reason of ecclesiastical ineptitude. The want of a lay element of ability and experience in the affairs of the university would probably have been fatal to its success were there no other and yet more formidable obstacles. Of these the chief was the usurpation by the episcopal committee of parental and national rights as real and important as their own. It was pointed out, in a former letter, that the authority in education was not single but dual. While the Bishop has the supreme right of veto, while he has the duty, belonging essentially to his office, of seeing that the intellectual cultivation of the pupil proceeds without danger or detriment to his faith, the parent has an equal right to decide what the kind and extent of that cultivation shall be. Were these rights ever acknowledged? Were the Irish people, or any person or persons who could be fairly held to represent them, ever consulted about the arrangement of a curriculum, or the appointment and payment of professors in the late university? And if not, was not the omission, the usurpation on the part of this board of a right not truly theirs? Insisting as I do on the supremacy of the Church in the school, I insist with equal emphasis on the educational right and duty of the parent which existed before the Church was.* From the authorities we hear nothing of these, yet I venture to assert that the scandalous and almost hopeless muddle into which the whole question has got has its origin in their violation. On this as on other points we want teaching and leading; we get neither.

In a late pastoral Cardinal McCabe appealed to history for evidence of the priceless services rendered by the Church to society. He recalled the fact of the Pope marshalling Europe against the Turk, and thereby saving it from barbarism. The Cardinal clearly sees how dangerous was the barbarian of the middle age; he is blind to the nature of the barbarian at his own gate. He makes peace and alliance with this man, more dangerous because more educated and more cunning than the Turk. He has no word of remonstrance or condemnation for the Yorkshire savage who so lately worked his brutal will in Ireland; nor has the "gentle and firm" Spencer anything to apprehend from his censure. No warning voice is raised—no marshalling Christian Ireland against the enemy, threatening its physical as well as its spiritual life. He censures

---

* "Children have from their parents three things—existence, support, and education." . . . "The right of a parent to educate his child is the most sacred of all rights." . . . "The obligation founded in nature which binds a parent to educate his child binds him to educate him religiously." . . . "The natural law makes the parent responsible for the education of his child." . . . "The commission of the Church, therefore, is strictly limited to a definite end. As to letters, arts, and sciences, she has no more direct commission to teach them to children than she has to teach trades and prefessions to adults." . . . "The Church intervenes to teach religion and morals; and she does this in perfect harmony with the natural right." (St. Thomas, quoted by the Bishop of Salford in his pamphlet, "Parental Right and Church Government in Education.") In this we have laid down, by the greatest of authorities, the principle that the greater part of the work of education is parental, and should be begun and conducted by the laity. The parent, in education, creates the body ; the Church infuses the soul ; and neither work is complete without the other. •

the false history of the past, while he favours in the present the falsest
of current historians and the meanest libeller of his people, a journal
so utterly mercenary that it does not so much as pretend to be guided
by any principle, or to sustain any policy save what subserves its own
interest.* And, accordingly, we find this detestable print in the hands or
on the tables of the Dublin clergy to the exclusion of the national and
Catholic press. The Cardinal goes on in this pastoral to detail certain
Catholic disabilities and proceeds: "Thanks to the justice and good
sense of modern statesmanship, our educational grievances have been to
a large extent removed." Will his Eminence condescend to say who are
the statesmen, and when the justice and good sense have been shown?
Why is there no word of acknowledgment to Mr. Parnell and the Irish
party who gained the "concessions"—such as they are? He goes on:
"Meanwhile, till the full measure of educational justice is dealt out to
us—which with God's blessing and our own exertions will be soon"—
may we further inquire what is this "full measure," who is to make the
exertions, and what form the movement is to take? This is eminently
a case in which God will help those who help themselves, and in which
action, bold and uncompromising, is worth all the vague rhetoric that
could be written. "Great educational victories," the Cardinal adds,
"have been already won, and in God's good time the unfinished work
of justice will soon be completed." Again the question arises: what
are the "victories?" who won them? and is the finishing of the "work
of justice" to be the granting of more money to the Royal University?

It is impossible to discuss this pastoral as it deserves, since to do so
would make one seem to be wanting in respect to the writer. We pass
from it with the remark that it leaves, after careful study, a painful
sense of deficiency. No claim is made, no plan suggested, no movement
advised—all is indefinite and shadowy, save the intention to trust to
"the justice of our rulers." Until his Eminence gets rid of this latter
hallucination he will never effect any good for Ireland, educational or
otherwise. Relying on it now, he says in effect, "Shut your eyes and
open your mouth and see what Dublin Castle will send you." But what
is to be deprecated most in this pastoral is the absence of any warning
against or denunciation of the atheistic principle now at the beginning
and end of our educational system. The apparent acceptance of this
comdemned compromise favours the idea that until the education
question has been removed from the present hands no real advance can
be made. There is apparent on the part of his Eminence a total
insensibility to the popular feeling—a want of touch with his people as
extraordinary as it is dangerous in one of his exalted and responsible
position. He refers to the "distinguished Rector of the Catholic Univer-

* The *Irish Times*.

sity." The same school that is already gazetted as defunct. It is better to be plain in matters of such moment. No movement in advance can or will be made as long as that gentleman is in the front. He is one of the three ecclesiastics in Ireland most obnoxious to popular feeling. There is not a man living worthy of the name of Irishman who would trust him with the education of his son—taking the word in its highest sense. Let me be just: he is a man of great abilities and acquirements, an adept in science, and an accomplished player of lawn tennis. The former qualities are voided by the direction Castlewards given to them; while, as. to the latter, they may be useful and agreeable in their way, but not quite those needed in a man who would undertake the weightest and grandest task conceivable. This is to create from the intellectual wealth of Ireland the chiefs of a new order, the conquerors of a more dangerous barbarism than the old, because it is apostate from true civilisation. The Rev. Dr. Gerald Molloy may keep the science for the "Royal" and the lawn tennis for the "Squares." He may be well assured that they make no claim for him to guide the Catholic University of the future. Very different must be the man who will undertake the sacred duty of banishing from the higher mind of Ireland West Britonism, and Castleism, and worldliness, and replacing these by the Christian Idea, with its wealth of virtues, natural and supernatural, especially with an enlightened patriotism. This noble virtue is the very antithesis of everything associated with the Rev. Doctor, as well as with his predecessor, the Dean of Cork, and all the unhappy roll of Castle ecclesiastics. Greatest of natural virtues, it has a faith, hope, and charity of its own, which almost ranks it with the supernatural, and makes it capable of producing in the social order results analogous to those of the supernatural virtues in the spiritual. The "Distinguished Rector" lately addressed a long report to the Bishops assembled at Maynooth. (By the way, on this occasion, their lordships issued no manifesto of the usual unreal kind.) It was mainly concerned with the shortcomings of the Queen's Colleges, against which he drew a heavy indictment, and then passed on to the recital of the successes of the various Catholic Colleges, which he spoke of as members of a Catholic University of which he was the head. If the inquiry be not impertinent, we would like to know what connection the doctor has with Tullabeg, or Blackrock, or St. Colman's, or Carlow? Has he become director of their studies, or have they authorised him to speak in their name? To simple people the elaborate address of the "Distinguished Rector," *apropos* of nothing particular, seems little better than trifling with the gravest of subjects, or an attempt to throw dust in the eyes of the public to cover a retreat and a failure.

To sum up: Our whole educational system needs instant reformation, and a good deal yet to be "improved" out of existence. There is the "National" School, void of the history and the religion of the people; the model school to which the Catholic child may not go; the Queen's Colleges, hastening to an unregretted and unhonoured dissolution; and the Catholic Colleges (with the Schools of the Christian Brothers, the only teaching institutions formed and conducted on true principles) affiliated to a Godless Examining Board (miscalled a University), with an Orange Freemason for its Chancellor! This is a spectacle which Catholic Ireland should not tolerate any longer. Of all this scandalous confusion the Castle Bishop is the cause, and it will require very different men from our Dean Nevilles and Dr. Molloys to change and end it.

I am,

AN IRISH CATHOLIC LAYMAN.

GENESIS OF THE CASTLE BISHOP.

THROUGH whatever recondite mode of evolution he may have come down to us, the Castle bishop was originally a bishop of the Pale. He it was who framed laws against the admission of Irish clerics or religious into benefices or abbeys under his control, who failed, in their regard, in every manifestation of charity. Nor does he seem to have taken much concern to reform the thieving and murderous propensities of his subjects, when the objects of their attention were Irish lands or Irishmen.

A common persecution and mutual danger subsequently made him nominally one with his Irish coadjutors, and though he occasionally showed his origin in his mode of meeting these, and in his tenderness for the common enemy, he was not on the surface much distinguishable from his fellows. The moment, however, any relaxation of the penal statutes was forced on the persecutor he began to preach "loyalty" and confidence in "the good intentions of our rulers." When Emancipation came, it found him ready to attorn to the Castle, and to declare that the English Government in Ireland was the best of all possible Governments in the happiest of all possible countries, if only the unreasonable natives would look at things as he saw them. He was always ready to maintain that the English wolf was really a most considerate and benevolent animal, and the Irish lamb a most perverse and ungrateful beast, who would not be quiet and respond to the good feeling and good intentions so constantly shown by *Lupus*. This may look like a mild joke, but it is nevertheless a sad and serious truth, as all know who are familiar with the Castle bishop's ways during this century.

The English Government stands openly convicted at this moment of
a comprehensive scheme for "improving" the Irish people out of Ireland
to the frozen wastes of Canada, or Manitoba—or elsewhere. It stands
openly convicted of aiding by encouragement and connivance the Orange
assassins in Ulster. These may incite to violence of the most dangerous
kind. They may commit murder by firing on a peaceful procession of
unarmed men. The forces of the Crown and the Royal Irish look on
and make no move to prevent or arrest them. Magnanimous and long-
suffering when his fellows of the Pale are on one side and the "mere
Irish" on the other, the Castle bishop never falters in his allegiance. Of
inexhaustible patience and charity where the enemy is in question, he is
ready to condone by silence, or, if necessary, to defend openly the most
violent and brutal excesses of "our rulers," while he publishes to the world
and condemns—let us grant, with righteous indignation—the crimes of the
people, which are the natural and almost necessary outcome of these
excesses. Short of personal violence offered to himself—say, imprison-
ment, under the Act, for intimidating his own priests, "to prevent them
doing what they have a legal right to do"—nothing conceivable could
open the eyes of the Castle bishop to the true nature of his friends.

To what is this portent due? How is it possible that men of high
station, great learning, great piety, and undoubted good intentions, are
blind to what to the rest of their countrymen is as clear as the sun at
noonday? How do they not see that the world (theologically meant) in
Ireland is like the world elsewhere—one of the deadliest enemies of God,
and accursed by Him ; and that there is, the earth round, no such incar
nation of this world given over to perdition as that Government with
which he has entered into friendly alliance.

If one might without being accused of profanity make a
comparison, the intimacy of some Catholic ecclesiastics with the
late "Buckshot" Secretary can be compared to nothing more
appositely than to the Prince of the Apostles calling on Pontius
Pilate, after the consummation of the crime at which creation
shuddered, to have some friendly talk and such refreshment as
was the fashion of the day. We have a notion of what the early
Christians would have thought of the (impossible) occurrence. Does the
Castle ecclesiastic know how his intimacy with the Pontius Pilate of
to-day is regarded by his people?

The ingenious theory of "P.K." will not explain the portent, for the
Castle priest is made by the Castle bishop, and the Castle layman is
mainly the outcome of both. We must, in the absence of a more
scientific theory, fall back on his descent, intellectually, from the
ecclesiastic of the Pale. We are further justified in supposing that his

incapacity to see the falseness and danger of his position arises thus : Before an Irish Catholic ecclesiastic can voluntarily associate himself with the Castle he must be cursed with a natural obliquity of vision. Once he attorns to the seat of iniquity, once he passes the fatal portals, dementia seizes him, and repentance and reform become impossible.

There is, however, in the communion of the Castle bishop and his associates an action and reaction which, if it does not account for the origin of the phenomenon, sufficiently explains its intensity. The chief personage in the "respectable Cawtholic" society of Dublin is the placeman, and pre-eminently the judge. He is in the inner circle. He forms part of that which is our curse. He touches, or is supposed to touch, the springs of Government, though he no more guides the machine than (I envy the originator of the appropriate simile) the tail wags the dog. To him is drawn the Catholic barrister, the attorney, the doctor ; and after these the wealthier merchants and traders whose wives and daughters ambition the Castle. This is the shrine of their most fervent worship, and they have been often known to serve at it to the ruin of their fortunes and the loss of their souls. Put in with these the "Catholic" Privy Councillors, W. H. F. Cogan, The O'Conor Don, Christopher Talbot Redington—worthy son of the Sir T. N. Redington of Papal aggression times—with the few families of the Catholic gentry who reside permanently or occasionally in Dublin, and you have the lay elements of Catholic society.

Into this the Catholic ecclesiastic enters. If he be an Irishman, true grit, it will soon expel him. If he be one of the class " P.K." evidently knows and describes, he is soon lost to "faith and fatherland." He associates with men who, whatever their outward seeming, must be essentially worldly, selfishly ambitious, and politically corrupt. He joins their conversations, eats their good dinners, drinks their fine wines, and becomes like to them. What can he know or care about the starving peasant in Connaught ? He does not seem to know of the traffic in Catholic souls carried on in the Liberties. *In Dublin the world has entered the sanctuary.* With the ecclesiastic of the ordinary type, if " position " be not everything, it goes for a great deal. It is a hard saying, but it is true ; and it accounts for many things it may be necessary by-and-by to detail, and which would be otherwise unaccountable. So insidiously and powerfully does this Cawtholic society act on those who court it, that the late Archibishop of Tuam is reported to have said that he would not trust himself to live a fortnight in it and expect to retain the clearness and strength of his convictions.

The effect of this corrupt and corrupting society on religion is most lamentable. The writer has been told by a priest of great experience that the morals of Catholic Dublin have declined twenty-five per cent in a single generation. There is no city of its size in the empire where so many young men go wrong. In no town of Great Britain does the hideous vice of great cities flaunt itself so audaciously and so publicly. No street or square is too respectable for its exhibition. It seats itself on the very steps of the metropolitan palace. Now, in every state of society this abomination must exist; but it need not be permitted to spread itself like a cancer over the face of the city when darkness draws forth its hated presence. This I take to be one of the outcomes of the Castle alliance; since this latter destroys, ere it has birth, all public, manly spirit in our youth. Patriotic associations, all that could give elevation of aim and active interest in public affairs, are by the Castle alliance barred and banned, and, when possible, suppressed. In the Catholic Commercial Club, numbering over 800 members, you may smoke and drink, play billiards and cards, but you must not discuss public affairs, and this rule is enforced by espionage. Deprived of everything to give them solidity and earnestness, the youth of Dublin betakes itself to the bars and music-halls, and then elsewhere. There is an immense amount of Catholic practice in Dublin; little of Catholic principle or Catholic public spirit. There is, in fact, often in the most unexpected places the densest ignorance of the teaching of the Church. The writer met lately a lawyer of good character as a Catholic, a county court judge, who stoutly defended Freemasonry, and maintained his right to hold his own opinion regarding this "laudable and benevolent" institution.

This non-Catholic spirit has some wonderful developments. The ordinary and salutary duty of parochial visitation seems entirely neglected. Numbers of middle-class families there are, who have resided for years in the same houses, who have never had a priest inside their door. The writer can answer for one family which has never seen the face of its *parochus* or his representative, and whose only visitants in the ecclesiastical order were a Presbyterian minister, who called to see if haply it belonged to him, and a Scripture reader, who asked permission to "read a chapter." Poor creatures! they were earning their living; but where was the true shepherd—he whose duty it was to know his flock one by one, as he has to answer for the least of their souls? This refers to a respectable locality. And if it be so in better-class streets, what must it be in the squalid garrets, and noisome cellars,

> "Where misery pours its hopeless groan,
> And weary want retires to die?"

Again, it is a hard saying, but it seems that if you are in Dublin a "carriage person" or a "Castle person," your soul may be thought worth looking after; but if you happen to be a common trader, you can save it or lose it, as you may elect, for all that is done by its guardian. How can he answer for his charge? How can he count them every one, and watch lest the wolf enters, when he does not even know them? In many other ways the Catholic spirit of Dublin is thoroughly demoralised. It will not soon be forgotten how lately a convent of regular ecclesiastics refused to cast the votes which would have returned a majority of Catholic guardians for the North City Union. The first effect of this *quasi* apostasy was to put an Emergency marine, without training or experience, for master over two thousand Catholic paupers; and to repeal the Emancipation Act as far as they were concerned.* Did these fathers reflect that it would depend frequently on the votes they refused whether unhappy children, foundlings or orphans, would or would not be brought up in the true faith of Christ; and that in the latter contingency they became directly answerable?

During the late trials in Dublin the Emancipation Act was for the general public likewise practically repealed. The proceedings were like what used to pass in Tipperary during the land war of forty years ago. A landlord or agent was shot. Forthwith someone was arrested—the right man if there was evidence sufficient; the likeliest man, in the eyes of the authorities, if that was not available. But so surely as anyone charged with such crimes went before the Orange landlord jury "well and truly" packed in Clonmel, so surely was he convicted and hanged. It was justice if that could be enacted; it was vengeance if justice was not attainable. So in the late murder trials in Dublin. The guilt of Francis Hynes, of Poff and Barret, of Walsh and Myles Joyce, was certainly not proved. Their innocence is believed in by nine-tenths of the Irish people—and, indeed, in more than one of the cases has been tentatively admitted by the Government. These men were done to death, not for the ends of justice, but to satisfy the craving for vengeance of the governing class. The conviction of these men was obtained by the most flagrant jury-packing. Now, the jurors were not necessarily perjurers or murderers. This theory is not necessary to brand with infamy the executive, which put in the box not twelve men "impartially chosen," but twelve violently prejudiced against the prisoners. One of the sayings which escaped the secrecy of the jury-room and nearly caused another death ("hang them all") is significant of the temper in which the life or death of the prisoners was discussed. By no straining of language could the trials be called fair. A drumhead court-martial would be fairer because honester. The form of law would not be used while its spirit was perverted. The constitution would not be outraged because

---

* This person has since been dismissed.

II

not invoked. Emancipation was repealed for the time, and Catholic Dublin made no sign. It permitted justice and freedom and national and Catholic principles to be outraged, and with ineffable meanness and cowardice made nor reclamation nor remonstrance. The *Freeman* suggested a meeting to show some sense of the ignominy put on the city. It elicited no answer; and an un-Irish and un-Catholic and slavish silence was observed because our chiefs were in alliance with the Castle.

Worse remains. Whatever may be said of Dublin in other respects, it could never be charged with want of generosity. In proportion to their means, all classes answer munificently to every call for religion or charity. What, then, can be said in extenuation or excuse of the proselytising of hundreds of Catholic children in the Coombe and other Souper schools? The traffic in souls, put down midst the misery of the West, has found place in Dublin. The *Freeman*, most optimist of journals when ecclesiastics of high rank are concerned, was compelled to ask "who's to blame?" when the facts were disclosed. Well, the *Freeman* knows who and what is to blame. Some spasmodic attempts have been since made to cope with this awful scandal, but we have seen none of that righteous indignation which would have raised Dublin as one man to reclaim these poor abandoned children and stay the ravages of the traffickers in souls. Dublin ecclesiastics sometimes give the rein to critical and supercilious remarks on their country brethren, but they must bear to be told that in no diocese in Ireland but the Metropolitan could Mrs. —— and the Irish Church Mission buy in such startling numbers the souls of destitute Catholic children. It is all of a piece. It all results from "coming to terms with modern civilisation," and entering into alliance with the enemy of the Irish people and of God. The Castle ecclesiastic is incessantly engaged digging a gulf between himself and his people. It is not the latter who will fall into it. At the O'Connell Centenary, at the opening of the Exhibition, the Irish democracy found itself deserted by its leaders, secular and ecclesiastic. It will go on without them—it will achieve its just and lawful aims. On the deserters be the blame of all the danger and evil (which may God avert!) which may come of the desertion. The Cardinal might rule in Dublin. He might organise his people as one man, and reign with a power never possessed by mediæval prince-bishop—a power founded on their inviolable faith and self-sacrifice. He prefers to abandon them. His influence declines to naught. I repeat, there are tens of thousands in Dublin who, God aiding them, would give their lives for the faith, who will not enter a church where their chief pastor presides, nor read a line which he writes. His warmest friends could not advise a public reception when he returned clothed with the cardinalitial dignity. What does the Castle give him to repay the loss of his faithful people's confidence—what to counterbalance the weakening of faith, the lowering tone of morals, the proximate danger, if not loss of souls? What for the destruction of the unity of the Church in Ireland, and the paralysis of its influence for all Irish and Catholic ends? Better ask the questions now than ask them too late.

AN IRISH CATHOLIC LAYMAN.

THE CASTLE BISHOP: HIS ALLIES AND HIS END.

SIR, Reviewing the personage who has so long occupied our attention, it occurs to me to ask: Does he know the century he lives in? does he know the time of day? does he know the people with whom he has to deal? To all these questions a negative answer must be given, since to answer affirmatively would be to accuse him of practical apostacy.

It is one of the misfortunes of our condition that there is in Ireland no highly educated zealous Catholic upper class which in social intimacy would mingle with our spiritual chiefs and give them some idea of what the outside world is thinking and saying. In Irish society our Catholic aristocracy occupy something of the position of the Eurasian in India, or the " mean whites " of the late slave States of the American Union ; that is, they are an invertebrate, contemptible lot, entirely without influence or consideration, despised by their enemies and abhorred by the people of whom they should have been leaders and protectors.* As it is, the wholesome breath of public opinion seldom disturbs the serenity of the episcopal palace. In the conference meetings, where frankness and courage would be of immense value, these qualities are not often met with ; and it not unfrequently happens that the cleric who is most prompt to declaim against his chief in his absence, in his presence sits dumb.

Dwelling in the atmosphere of the Castle or the squares, or separated from his priests and his people by an unwise and ill-timed exclusiveness, the Castle bishop sees nothing of the outer world, and therefore learns nothing. History has no light for him, and the most patent facts of contemporary life teach him nothing. He might see, if he would, the rapid change in the world around—that change which brings, with so many other things of good and evil, a universal spirit of inquiry and criticism, which, whatever its tendency, has to be met and dealt with as a fact. Before this spirit everything of prescription and privilege is melting away. No claim of immunity not deriving directly

---

* Since this was written, we have the full text of the new patent extermination scheme, signed by J. Ross, of Bladensburgh, and Christopher Talbot Redington!

from God, no assertion of authority not clearly and logically provable, will prevail against its keen and rigid test. The Irish people are, thank God, by a miracle of his grace, still a faithful people, but they are no more the people of fifty, or forty, or even thirty years ago than if two centuries had rolled between. The bartering of every Irish and Catholic interest by the late Cardinal to make John Sadleir a Lord of the Treasury and William Keogh a judge would be no more possible now than the restoration of the Established Church. The time is rapidly coming when the Irish people will make any complicity or collusion between their spiritual chiefs and the hypocrites and frauds who pretend to fulfil in their regard the duties of governors equally impossible.

If the Castle bishop took thought of what goes on in any country in Europe he would quickly change his mode. In the Peninsula the Church daily loses ground. In France she is crucified between the indifferentism of her nominal children and the unrestrained hostility of her enemies. In Germany she is under the heel of Bismarck. In Italy, in Rome itself, she is the sport of the Revolution. In this country—the only spot in Europe, in the world, where she might reign—the Castle bishop blindly and wantonly casts to the winds the priceless blessing, and throws away opportunities of good beyond compare. Many a French bishop would give half the years allotted to him to lead a people so docile, so self-sacrificing, so prompt to respond to any call of duty and of faith, as any Irish bishop can command.

How long they will remain so who can tell? One thing is certain— miracles are not the normal condition of life, and no people ever did or ever could stand always the strain put upon his flock by the Castle bishop. Better to say now, while there is yet time, that in the new Ireland being reconstituted before our eyes there is no place for him, than to let him go on, till he is awakened too late by the sight of an alienated people, failing to discriminate between his person and his office, and rejecting both because believing both to be hostile. "If ever," said the saintly oracle which spoke but of late from Tuam, "the Irish people separate from the Irish Church it will not be the fault of the people."

Thank God, it is not as yet the Irish people who are separating from the Church, but the Castle bishop who separates himself from the people. What is this people from whom he separates himself? Surely the noblest of the whole human family, since they have preserved the first attributes of humanity under difficulties never experienced by any other. "Whatever," says the great English moralist, "raises us above the power of the senses—whatever makes the past, the distant, and the future predominate over the present —advances us in dignity as human beings." In his squalid cabin the

Irish peasant is raised by faith above the degrading power of sense ; the tradition of a glorious past is for him a living voice ; his kin in distant America or Australia animate him with ever-renewed fortitude and courage ; and the future is bright with an undying hope of the speedy coming of that day which will see him restored to happiness in his own land.   Few in numbers, contemptible in resources, the Irish people have carried on for ages the struggle for national right and human freedom against the most powerful, the most unprincipled, the most remorseless of nations.   And in the course of the struggle they have never claimed anything that was not right and just.   They are conquering by the power of sacrifice, and slowly but certainly forcing their enemy to plead before the bar of public opinion, and to withdraw the infamous slanders by which his tyranny was sought to be justified.   The Irish people deserve well of civilization, since there is no department of human activity or achievement which has not been illustrated by their sons. They have given to Europe, to America, to Australia, statesmen, warriors, and legislators.   But lately three men of Irish descent—Mac Mahon in France, O'Donnell in Spain, and Nugent in Austria—ruled three of the greatest States in the world.   They have been in every clime pioneers of progress.   The chief builders of the Australian empire are Irishmen. In the old world as in the new thousands of altars are dedicated under the names of their saints.   Above all, this martyr nation has held aloft for three centuries the banner of the Cross, and exhibited to the world a people faithful to death for conscience' sake, holding lands and property and life as nothing in comparison with the priceless treasure with which their very name has become synonymous.   And all this in an age which has made a god of this world, and which places things of sense first and things of the Spirit nowhere.

In his highest example, the Irishman ranks with the first of the human family.   In his lowest he is no less remarkable.   You see the Connaught peasant at his cabin door, not seldom excavated from the bog; or return his salutation as he passes on the road.   Ragged, unkempt, often broken with toil, bearing in his features the stamp of centuries of starvation, to the worldling he is an object of contempt or dislike ; to the eye of faith, one of respect approaching to veneration.   For he is almost certainly the descendant of martyrs, and is a confessor in his own person.   He realises, in a manner not known to more favoured nations, the strength and purity of the family tie, the sanctities of the Christian home.   By taking his child by the hand to the Souper School, or giving himself the barest outward compliance with the preposterous heresy which is always on the watch to purchase souls, he could change in a moment his lot of extremest hardship to one of comfort and even luxury. Yet Souperism, after a transient and very partial success, has utterly failed in Ireland. In the town of Clifden, where £20,000 has been poured out for twenty years, not one family belonging to the mission is found, the only non-Catholic family in the town being respectable Presbyterians, who don't acknowledge the Soupers. And this is the man whom the Castle bishop would deliver, bound and gagged, to his enemies !

What is this which the Castle bishop abandons and betrays ? Surely

> "The noblest cause that tongue or sword
> Of mortal ever lost or gained."

Of this cause and its leader the poet might have still more truly, though not more eloquently, written :—

> "Forth from its scabbard never hand
> Waved sword from stain as free,
> Nor purer soul led a braver band,
> Nor braver toiled for a brighter land,
> Nor brighter land had a cause more grand,
> Nor cause a chief like thee."

Coming down to us through eight centuries, it embraces every element of human interest, of racial origin, of history, of politics, of religion. At this moment it is complicated by others, social and industrial, and, above all, by the struggle for possession of the land, on which all others finally turn and rest. Who wins in the last particular wins all along the line. History shows nothing comparable to it. A people, I repeat, few in number, and deprived of all the ordinary elements of power, maintaining a struggle of centuries against a conquering and dominating race with command of all the "resources of civilisation," and wielding these with an unscrupulousness and ferocity unparalleled— winning, at last, by an inviolable adherence to principle and an invincible patience and constancy. This is a spectacle as unique as it is invaluable. The statesman can draw from it lessons of priceless value ; the poet, inspiration for his muse's highest flight ; the Catholic publicist confirmation of every principle he advocates ; the patriot of every clime, strength and courage to continue his struggle to the end. No other cause since the world began so exhibits all justice, all truth, all right on the one side, all injustice, all falsehood, all wrong at the other. This cause it is which the Castle bishop, with a blindness and fatuity incredible if they were not palpable, abandons and betrays. When his people, in despite of him, emancipate themselves from the Orange, Freemason, anti-Christian ring which represses their every movement of national and religious life (and endeavours to exasperate them into resistance to effect their ruin), he will see his frightful error. God grant he will not see it too late.

So strangely constituted is our nature that its very virtues often issue in defect. The Castle bishop in the past owed his immunity and his power for evil to the profound respect for the ecclesiastical order which is one of the outcomes of the vivid faith of the Irish people. An anti-English bishop would not be possible in England, nor an anti-French one in France, nor an anti-Italian one in Italy. The time has come when an anti-Irish bishop will be no longer possible in Ireland. The universal spread of education, the penetration of the National press to the remotest parts, the formation of correct and enlightened opinions as to the true relations of the Church to the people, will make his existence much longer impossible. His ever having been can neither be explained nor understood ; for if, as Dr. Croke asserts, "The religion and nationality of Ireland are inseparable"—if, as Cardinal Newman teaches, "They (the Irish) mingle nationality with religion, and religion with nationality ;" and, again, "No one can tell in Irish affairs when religion ends and nationality begins." If all this be true, and the Irish people know it to be true, the Castle bishop in joining the enemies of Ireland allies himself with the enemies of God and of His Christ. If there be on earth one place above all others where "the world, the flesh, and the devil" are incarnated, it is Dublin Castle. Its rule in Ireland is what Mr. Gladstone said in relation to Naples—"The negation of justice, which is the negation of God." The Castle bishop, in going to it, in adopting its ideas, in upholding its policy, utterly ruins his authority with his people, goes back on all the truths he is commissioned to teach, and puts in peril, as far as he individually can, the faith and morals of his people.

In the beginning of these letters I inquired, "How long is the Castle bishop to be tolerated in Ireland ?" I had intended to propose a scheme by which, without any violation of Catholic principle or Catholic feeling, his end would be hastened. It will keep and gain force by the keeping. In any case it would be better proposed by an ecclesiastic ; and probably there will be found some one self-sacrificing and patriotic enough to undertake the duty. In the meantime we of the laity have a right to demand that the scandalous division of the Irish hierarchy (of which the Castle bishop is the cause) shall cease. For it is notorious that this threatens the very existence as well as the faith of the Irish people This division is not only on matters of principle, as on the education question, but on matters of policy touching the life of the nation. The Castle bishop may take some warning from various signs which even he cannot overlook. It may be in your memory, sir, that many years ago, and more than once, I proposed to deal with this question, and asked your permission to use the columns of the *Nation* to point out that the deadliest enemies of Ireland were the Castle bishop and the dry rot of Whiggery in the Irish Church. This permission was then emphatically refused; and your granting it now is evidence of a prodigious advance in public opinion. The last *Irish Monthly* has a letter from Gavan Duffy to D'Arcy McGee, warning the latter not to touch the question under penalty of being ruined. That a layman—"wholly deficient," as the Cardinal truly observed, "in theological science"—should now, at the suggestion and with the approval of distinguished ecclesiastics, undertake the exposition and defence of the Christian order in Irish society against the Castle bishop is evidence of a change which even he cannot overlook. He has gone one step too far. As long as he contented himself with crossing and defeating every Irish and Catholic movement he might have been tolerated. When he goes to the heart of our spiritual life, and endeavours to make the Holy Father a party against us, it is time to take action against him. For until he is made impossible the relations of Ireland with the Holy See will be in peril.—I am, sir, yours, &c.,

AN IRISH CATHOLIC LAYMAN.

THE CASTLE BISHOP AND THE ENGLISH CATHOLIC FACTION.

SIR,—The preceding letters would be incomplete without some reference to one of the chief supports of our subject in his unhappy course. Mr. Errington may or may not be an imbecile fop. He derives his position before the public and his power for evil from the fact that he is held to represent a section of English Catholic opinion influential at Rome. It is this which gives our anti-Irish bishops their predominance. It is freely said that Cardinal Howard's least word would prevail against the strongest representations of any number of Archbishops of Cashel or Bishops of Meath, even though the subject was one of which the latter were the true and proper judges, and the former could by no possibility have any true notion. We are bound, therefore, to endeavour to get some idea of what this English faction really is; and I use the word faction to indicate a part and not the whole body of English Catholics for this contains many men as ardent lovers of Ireland as they are truly Catholic. Unfortunately they do not appear to be able to leaven the mass or to make their ideas prevail. We are none of us pure intelligences. We are, everyone, coloured by the atmosphere we breathe, and influenced more or less by our surroundings. Only a genius or a saint rises superior to these—the first because he is a genius, and penetrates to the nature of things through their outward guises; the latter because he draws his inspiration from heaven. Now, the one character or the other has never been common in the world, and perhaps never so uncommon as to-day. The average Briton, therefore, has as little chance of seeing the truth of things Irish as a man would have of seeing natural objects properly through glass stained red, or blue, or yellow. He has, if he would acquire a true knowledge of Irish affairs, to penetrate a tradition of falsehood of seven centuries' growth, to clear his mind of a cloud of prejudice forced in upon it by everything he reads and hears in his daily life, and to confess himself a member of a community which has exhausted against an unoffending people the whole range of human crime, which still does all the evil it is permitted to do, and with an amazing audacity claims credit for not doing that which is no longer possible. It is evident that all this is far beyond the power of the person in question; and instead of being surprised at the stupid malice we see so often displayed in our regard, we should rather be thankful that there are some few Englishmen who grasp the realities of the Irish question, and advocate its true solution.

The average British Catholic is, in Irish affairs, an Englishman first, and a Catholic after. He never reads an Irish Catholic or national paper. I met lately a friend, an English ecclesiastic of high position, and almost before the ordinary greeting was over, he literally burst into a tirade of abuse against Parnell and Davitt, and the Irish movement generally. While he was exhausting himself, I thought: Is it any use trying to enlighten this good man? and concluding it was not, replied never a word, and talked of the weather. Another priest on the London mission made, in the hearing of the writer, an extraordinary statement respecting an event which had just occurred. On being challenged for his authority, he replied: "Oh, I saw it in the *Times* and the speech of the Attorney-General." This gentleman would resent being called unfair and unjust, yet he goes for his facts to a hired slanderer, and to the most notorious and inveterate enemy of everything Irish.

This is the ordinary state of mind of the average Englishman— Catholic and Protestant, lay and cleric. It is created and supported by a thousand influences. It is upheld by a feeling of his own superiority, and of consequent contempt for the people who trouble his peace and rather damage him in the world's opinion. Not always consciously, there is yet at the bottom of his mind the notion that the Irish are an inferior people, and therefore defends the whole course of English rule in Ireland by "the right of conquest," which is pure paganism, and that their domination by the imperial race is part of the "eternal fitness of things."

Those who have had opportunities of comparing the two peoples in every one particular honourable to men may smile at this feeling, but it is a very real misfortune for us, since it is that which most constantly operates against the formation in England of a just public opinion. Whatever excuse or palliation there may be for the layman who yields willingly to the anti-Irish influence, there is none, it seems to me, for the cleric. For he is bound to weigh facts in the scale of the sanctuary. He is doubly bound as a teacher to know the truth. He should remember that English society is essentially pagan ; that its beginning was in an impious lie—the assertion that Henry VIII. and not the Pope was the Vicar of Christ ; that it is the outcome of a blasphemous rebellion against God and the Church of which he is a minister ; and that in its every development it shows daily clearer and clearer the evidence of its origin, and the doom to which it hastens. When he "comes to terms with modern civilisation," when he makes himself one with English society as it exists around him, he acts as the early Christians would have done had they entered into the society of pagan Rome and accepted its toleration, which is another way of saying that Christianity would have perished ere it arose.

In the whole controversy between the two countries the English view is worldly, corrupt, and pagan ; the Irish spiritual, just, Christian, Catholic. In adopting the former the English ecclesiastic makes himself, unconsciously though it be, one with the enemies of the Cross of Christ, and impedes with all his power the salvation of his country.

We will get a clearer view of the condition of English Catholicism if we take the *Tablet* as its representative. It is the more desirable to use this method, as it will enable us to reclaim against the part this once admirable journal has lately taken in Irish affairs. In the hands of Frederick Lucas it was a synonym for everything honest and straight-forward in policy, frank and manly in expression, elevated and noble in aim. For several years it has been the very reverse. Happily for us, its mental and moral decay have been coincident, and it is not now capable of doing the mischief its conductor apparently desires. Not that it is not edited with the gravity and care which become its proprietorship, and that its literary work does not at least attain a respectable mediocrity ; but as a journal claiming to be the chief representative of Catholic opinion in Great Britain it is utterly unworthy of the position— it is, in fact, below contempt. These are strong expressions, yet I hope to justify them before coming to an end.

The *Tablet* is owned by the Right Rev. Dr. Vaughan, Bishop of Salford, one of a family distinguished for great services to the Church. This eminent prelate is himself the ideal of an English bishop. Of a noble presence, genial and frank in disposition, accessible, urbane, courteous in manner, in ability and cultivation far beyond the average;

he bears himself with judgment and dignity before the great community midst which he moves. His administration of the diocese of Salford has been marked by a decided advance in Catholic affairs ; and if it has shown any deficiency it is only such as was inevitable from want of understanding the Irish portion of his flock.

In the paper owned by this great Catholic ecclesiastic the Catholic people of Ireland has found its most bitter, most false, most inveterate enemy.

That the bishop believes this no one who knows him (and to know is to venerate and love) can for a moment imagine. It is possible he does not read the paper at all. Certainly from it he has nothing to learn. It is certain also that he does not know the effects it produces. If he did we may well suppose he would quickly terminate his connection with it. If the *Tablet* would let us alone we might wonder, yet we would have no right to complain. It has not even that very negative merit : it takes sides against us. It is skilled in regard to Irish affairs in all the forms of the *suggestio falsi* and the *suppressio veri*, while occasionally it ventures on the lie direct with an audacity which rivals the *Times*. Long a leader in the conspiracy of silence, it has of late become a conspicuous member of the conspiracy of slander, and Father George Angus, or the recreant Bellingham, or anyone else who chooses to dip pen in gall to write about Irish men or things, has free scope in its pages. For defence, or explanation, or justification, there is no allowance : "they would cause discussion."

For sophistry, meanness, and falsehood, the *Tablet* on Irish affairs equals or surpasses any of its Protestant contemporaries. Everything favourable to the country is suppressed, everything unfavourable put forward. The result is that the presentation of the Irish question amounts to one gigantic falsehood. We are treated to such headings as, "A Week's Crime in Ireland," when a multitude of facts and reports of "facts" which never occurred are brought together to make a picture of repulsive darkness. At another time we have an article headed, "England and Ireland," showing the infinite forbearance and goodness of England and the utter perversity of Ireland. In a word, every fact, every principle, arising between the two countries, is reversed, and a reader drawing his information from the *Tablet* alone would be tempted to think Ireland and its people justly entitled to a place in the "Inferno."

To aggravate the injustice, the slander, the reversal of all truth in the controversy, the Papal approval granted to the *Tablet* when under very different management, and when its whole meaning was the reverse of what it is, still remains blazoned on its front. We have ample cause to feel indignant at this. We have a right to demand that the Holy

Father (for in this Leo the Thirteenth is Pius the Ninth) shall no longer be made a party to the rankest injustice, and that his sacred name and office shall not serve to cloak the basest forms of heretical pravity.

It needs no "scientific theologian" to extract from many of the later numbers of the *Tablet* propositions which, if not downright heretical, should be marked by the notes which describe the stages of approach to the sin of sins. The explanation may be found in this—that the editor is a half-converted British Philistine of the most inveterate type. He may have received the faith. I do not judge. It is clear from his work that his intellect (like the digestive organs of a late well-known convert) has never been converted. Now, we know that heresy has darkened the reason of the English people, and depraved and perverted their wills, and hence the scandals of relapses amongst converts, and the evident Protestant tone and sympathies of many who remain nominally Catholic. This will partly account for the course of the *Tablet*. Then, this editor is a toady and a tuft-hunter. He "dearly loves a lord." In his heart of hearts he has already canonised "the duke," and accords him at least the worship of *dulia*. To the aristocracy, generally, he bows down; and does his best to connect the Church of God with the cause of an effete and worthless class, which, in the judgment of every thinking man in England, is doomed to speedy destruction.

The claim of such a man to guide English opinion, Catholic or non-Catholic, is preposterous. His very highest aim seems to be "safe," and "respectable," and "genteel." He is so wholly in thrall to his feudal superiors that he does not scruple to suppress important items of English news when these might be unpleasant to the gods of his idolatry. For example, at the last meeting of the Catholic Union—which would be the chief organisation of English Catholicism if it was not smothered by rank and "respectability"—some gentlemen presumed to express the dangerous opinion that the Union should take action of one kind or another in public affairs. They were duly put down. A rift was made, however; some light was let in on the "masterly inaction" of our aristocratic chiefs; and, therefore, the *Tablet* suppressed the report altogether. The notes of its backslidings in Irish and Catholic affairs within, say, the last four years, would fill a small volume. Some few may here be named. It took up the defence of the "Kavanagh-Extermination-Replanting-with-Protestants" Society. It advocated Lord Derby's infamous suggestion of spending millions in "emigrating" the Irish people. It claimed honour and reward for Mr. Errington because he succeeded in imposing on Propaganda the English idea in all its infinite falsehood and injustice, and extracting the circular which Mr. Healy correctly described, and which will not be forgotten while its authors exist or the policy it indicates is pursued. To cap the climax of its iniquity, it has permitted, without a single word of condemnation, the advocacy in its columns of the eviction of the whole Irish people, on the ground that "it would pay." Yet this is the journal which writes of itself, "It is, therefore, now incumbent on the Catholic press of Europe, *which alone is swayed by the eternal principles of justice*, to raise its voice on behalf of the helpless and oppressed!" Therefore, we may presume, the *Tablet* was silent while its brethren in Ireland were victims of Buckshot's brutal tyranny: its strongest deprecatory phrase applied to one of his worst acts being that "it seemed rather arbitrary." Therefore, it rather approved of Lord Rossmore's assassination manifesto. Therefore it is on all occasions as ready as the Castle bishop to praise "the justice of our rulers," and anathematise all who stand against them. Again it is, we must suppose, because the *Tablet* "is swayed by the eternal principles of justice," that it had no word of condemnation for the Afghan or South African wars—perhaps the most wanton and iniquitous that England ever waged, or for the murdering of the Egyptians, with whom we were not at war at all. Arabi, to be sure, was, according to the *Tablet*, a "coward" and a "fanatic." "His ideas were incompatible with Western civilisation." Above all, his success in Egypt was adverse to "British interests," and therefore he must be squelched. Yet the *Tablet* could see that the French invasion of Tunis was a "monstrous iniquity!"

The whole thing is sickening. Glancing over the *Tablet*, we get a clear idea how the Reformation became possible in England, and how it could be made again. It was such wretched negations of everything robust, and honest, and Catholic which made it possible for a devil like Henry to destroy in a generation the work of a thousand years. If the class the *Tablet* represents were alone—if they did not themselves yield, as is likely, to the modern spirit, and become one with the world around them—they would be so handled by the Russell or the Gladstone of the day, as to quickly lose even the profession of Catholicism. For the people by whom they were emancipated, and by whom they are supported and protected, they have nothing but lying and slander, and the basest ingratitude.

An Irish Catholic Layman.

SOME NOTES ON ENGLISH CATHOLICISM.

Sir,—The sentence pronounced on the first transgression, if severe, was judicial. Uttered by a human tribunal, it would be intolerable, for it was for the bulk of mankind penal servitude for the years allotted to each, terminated by death. But infinite wisdom joined to it such compensations, as that no one who has tasted them would wish his lot other than it is. The sentence that man shall "earn his bread by the sweat of his brow" was not penal only. That which declares that, if "a man shall not work neither shall he eat," has two issues. If the "sweat" is given the "bread" is the just recompense. If a man is ready and willing to work he has a right to eat.

British law in Ireland has for generations denied to the people this primary and essential right. The Irish landlord has, indeed, in the past, commonly left his serf a bare subsistence in ordinary times ; but when pressure or scarcity came there was no reserve, and the serf begged or starved. An epitome of the whole Irish land system is found in the great Dillon estate in Mayo. This, which extends over 90,000 acres, was a century ago a waste of bog and moor. The gradual clearing of richer lands—the carrying out of the sentence, "To hell or Connaught"—gradually led to the settlement of this vast tract by squatters. The reclamation, such as it was, began, and also the rent. It is impossible to get at the earlier rent roll of the Dillon estate, but it is the general opinion, supported by the evidence of aged tenants, that fifty years ago it was between £10,000 and £11,000. It now stands at close on £30,000, the difference being the confiscated improvements of the tenantry. The process by which the advance was made can be compared to nothing but periodical blood-letting by a skilful surgeon. This does not threaten life; yet it so reduces the subject that, when the pressure of disease comes upon him, he yields at once. The late famine compelled three-fourths of the Dillon tenantry to appeal to the "Mansion House" or the "Duchess" relief funds, while the noble proprietor was not heard of. It is true indeed he was not getting his rents. How could he be when he got them ten times over in advance? If a man kills his goose he can't have the eggs also. The enormous rental yielded for so many years by this estate was largely produced by labour in England. The serf hired himself out for one-half the year to pay for the privilege of living for the other on Lord Dillon's bogs. The mansion house of Loughglynn has not known the presence of one of the title for forty years, nor has any appreciable portion of the vast revenue been spent in reproductive or any other works. The honey from this vast hive of 4,500 tenants was skilfully withdrawn, to be used or wasted elsewhere, and the toilers were left to starve.

When pressure of want roused the serfs to combination and resistance, the Lord Viscount was powerless. He could not evict nor consolidate. If the tenants were wise they could have made equitable terms. But they trusted to the honour of a

nobleman, and were deceived.   They went into the Land Courts.
Their lord asked them to withdraw the originating notices,
promising them the land at Griffith's valuation.   They did so;
and when the combination was broken up, and the Coercion Act introduced, he broke his promise in the fashion of any common dishonourable
mortal.   It would not be just to the well-known man who managed the
property for thirty years to omit saying that he retired from office some
three or four years ago.   A member of a much-respected Mayo family
then took it up; but finding the duties expected to be such as he could
not perform, he also withdrew; and finally a Mr. Murray Hussey was
imported from Kerry to do the needful.   This young person has been
made a "Jaa Pee," and the pranks he plays in the petty sessions courts
in his neighbourhood will probably be the subject of some questions in
the coming Parliament.   To repeat, the whole Irish land question is
epitomised in this one estate, and it is here particularised to give Lord
Dillon the publicity he merits, and the argument the solid foundation
of fact.   The Irish people claimed through the Land League the first of
all rights—the right to live by their labour.   The *Tablet*—English
Catholic paper—cried "confiscation," "robbery," "Communism."   The
Catholic people of Ireland demand to be freed from the domination of the
Orange-Freemason ring which tortures them.   The *Tablet* cries
"sedition."   It is said that it is a mere waste of time to expose this
paper—that no one reads it or cares what it says.   This I take to be a
mistake.   The paper may be intellectually contemptible.   But it has
behind it the great office and person of a Catholic bishop, and nothing
which appears in it can be void of the significance pertaining to this connection.   At lowest, the *Tablet* is the straw which shows the way the
wind blows, and how it became possible to obtain from Propaganda a
document so injurious and insulting to the Irish Church and people as
the late circular.

Whatever the editor be, it is time he was prevented from doing his
little best to hinder that cordial union of the Catholics of England with
us which must precede any solid advance, for them at least, on the line
of Catholic interests.

It is only too evident that obstacles enough to this union exist
already.   The English Catholic body seem struck with mortal paralysis
—intellectual and moral.   Thirty years ago it showed more activity and
life and hope than now.   We had then such men as Charles Langdale
(*clarum et venerabile nomen*) in Catholic public life, if not in politics.
Has he left no son to undertake the lapsed duties and perpetuate the
noble tradition?   We had Kenelm Digby painting with unrivalled
learning fascinating pictures of the ages of faith, and tracing

with wonderful skill the many roads of human life which lead
to the city of God. Does no man of his race exist to render the
pictures into realities, or show the way in one at least of the roads?
We had the venerable Charles Waterton illustrating what manner of
man it was who bore with such patient dignity the ostracism of
three centuries from the public life of that England his fathers had made;
the Waterton of to-day seems to exhaust himself in collecting editions of
a famous book written many centuries ago, and in endeavouring to
elucidate the hopeless problem of its authorship. Then there are Welds
and Maxwells, Stourtons and Scropes, Howards and Petres, with many
another, of whom it may be justly said that in personal qualities they
are worthy of their ancestry. What part do they take in the public life
of England—what action to stem the daily advance of paganism, or to
endeavour to restore the empire to the unity of Christendom? The
answer is their condemnation. There is not a single English Catholic
gentleman in the House of Commons; for it may be presumed that the
nondescript member for Berwick "don't count."

Yet this House of Commons is the centre and heart of our civilisation.
Who influences or guides it controls the destinies of the empire for good
or evil. Through it alone can the impulse be given which can effectually
raise or depress our national life. It is, therefore, of the first importance—
it is evidently essential—that a Catholic party be formed within it,
growing out of and acting with the Irish party. This could be easily
formed from the English Catholic gentry, for they have wealth, and
leisure, and cultivation. Two necessary qualities they have not, namely,
freedom from English prejudices, and the courage of their convictions.
They are, as has been said, in regard to Ireland, Englishmen first and
Catholics after. They have never shown, as regards public life, that
they had any conception of their duties, or the disinterestedness necessary
to the earlier stages of their fulfilment. It is no excuse to say they were
shut out from the representation of English constituencies by prejudice.
They could have got seats in Ireland in any necessary number. At
the next election twenty suitable men could get placed in the Irish
representation, but they would need to be very different from those we
have lately had a sample of. We don't want "clever idiots" like Lord
R. Montague, nor shams like the late Sir George Bowyer. We want
Frederick Lucases, if not in ability, at least in honesty and Catholic
spirit. Supposing the late Dr. Ward was as eloquent with tongue as
powerful with pen, what an unknown amount of good he could have
done in Parliament on such questions as education! His robust and
masculine understanding, displaying all that was best of the English
mind, would have given him the power of a party. It will yet be

recorded as evident proof of the decadence of the English Catholic body, that at the very turning-point of the history of both countries they have not given one man to do a man's work on the side of Catholic interests and public policy.

Enough there were on the other side. Mr. Gladstone, surely in this case a most credible witness, declared on bringing in the Compensation for Disturbance Bill that the lives of 15,000 Connaught peasants depended on its passing; that for them the sentence of eviction was a sentence of death. What did our English brethren in the faith care? At the head of the Catholic nobility, the Duke of Norfolk marched down to the Upper Chamber to vote the unroofing of three thousand humble homes, the quenching of as many hearths. Is his own rooftree the more secure, his own hearth the happier, for this callous and unchristian disregard of the interests of those who are most truly "*pauperes Christi?*" Does he think he has postponed for one day the inevitable question : What has he or what have his ancestors done to entitle him to levy a tax of a quarter of a million *per annum* on the industry of Sheffield? The Irish landlord stretched his claim beyond bearing. It has put him in the way of being deprived of what he is justly entitled to. And so the English aristocracy. They are riding on the very top of the law. The Marquis of Salisbury, who is as insolent and as selfish but rather more cunning than the rest of his class, begins to hearken to the "bitter cry of outcast London," but it will take more than words—it will take prompt heroic action—on his part, and on that of the Dukes of Bedford and Westminster, and the rest, if they are able to rescue their properties from the rising flood of lawless democracy—lawless, because it has for long been put by the feudal aristocracy out- side the law.

The English Catholic aristocracy, titled and untitled, have enormous interests at stake. The world around them moves with ever-increasing velocity, and they keep fiddling away, as did the French *noblesse* of the last century. With numberless practical questions calling for treatment and solution, their chief organ is filled with abstractions, such as essays on the " Days of Creation," the origin of the word "Mass," or the guilt or innocence of Mary of Scotland. Very interesting, no doubt, to a community in a satisfactory condition ; the merest trifling in face of such dangers and necessities as beset the Catholic Church in England. They might have a formidable party in both Houses of Parliament, looking after the administration of the poor-law, the care of Catholic orphans, the education question, and others equally pressing, while they are absolutely without voice or representation. They debate about Catholic action or inaction, and finally decide for the latter—their chief organisation, the Catholic Union, showing how "not to do it" in an incomparable

I

manner. We have suggestions of Catholic Liberal associations to form
a tail to the Whig party, and of Conservative ditto to form ditto to the
Tory party—one genius going the length of gravely proposing for the
latter the device of Tiara, Crown, and Bible, and for principal aim
the giving of an active support to the "present union of Church
and State in England." This is "our common Christianity" with a
vengeance. There is to be seen a good deal of intellectual activity
rarely directed to any useful purpose, and liberality sometimes more
scandalous than edifying. Thus the late Earl of Shrewsbury (O'Connell's
"pious fool") spent £100,000 on religious buildings at Alton and
Cheadle, rather monuments to his own glorification than as judicious
expenditure for Catholic purposes, while he could refuse a sovereign to a
good Scotch priest begging for a congregation of labourers.* The late
Sir W. Stewart, of Murthly, spent £30,000 on a private chapel, while a
few miles from his castle lived four hundred Irish Catholics without
church, or priest, or school. The Marquis of Bute gives years of labour
to the translation of the Breviary, and months to writing a life of St.
Mungo. Excellent and praiseworthy works is the noblest ambition that
ever inspired human activity was not open to him, namely, the reconstitution, in the Christian order, of the society of which he is so prominent
and powerful a member. This, his first and greatest duty, is so little in
his mind that, with an almost total want of Catholic middle-class and
university education before his eyes, he gave lately an enormous sum
(variously reported at from £40,000 to £60,000) to the Presbyterian
University of the wealthy city of Glasgow. Such an act as this may
well give rise to doubts as to the reality and permanency of his conversion, and to gravest fears for the future of a body of which he is one of
the principal "leaders." All this goes to prove that our English friends,
like some nearer home, "have come to terms with modern civilisation."
The outcome of recent long discussions is to leave the Church gagged
and bound, silent and degraded, before her enemy—the world. Not one
of the interlocutors gave a thought to the fact that there was a powerful
Catholic element here which would form the surest basis for any public
movement. Like the French Legitimists, the English Catholics seem to
be incapable, as regards public affairs, of anything but talking and
praying—excellent things when well done, and associated with prudent
and courageous action ; mere delusion without.

---

* This aged and exemplary priest still lives. When relating the circumstances of
his visit to Alton (the close of which was the shutting of his door by the noble earl
in the face of his visitor), he used to say, "That man's 'charities' will lose him his
soul." *Per contra*, he had, at nearly the same time, an experience of the opposite
kind. He was received at another noble house—Lord Stourton's, I think—with
gracious hospitality, compelled to stay overnight, and in the morning received the
offerings of the household, from the seniors to the youngest child of a large family,
and even the servants, who asked to be allowed to contribute.

For this incapacity, this nullity of public action, they have not one excuse. They have for leaders two men whose appearance marks an epoch*—one, chief of living men in the order of thought, the other as great in that of action. Of the latter, especially, the English Catholic body is not worthy. If the Irish people had the advantage of the leading wasted on men who will not follow, they would realise, as far as imperfect humanity can, and in a time incredibly short, that ideal which springs from a close and active union of the natural and supernatural. This day of all† others should inspire us with renewed energy, and a hope whose ardour is a presage of success. Our chief receives the homage of the nation he has emancipated anew. Before the world, in sight of all but those who will not see, he triumphs over his enemies and ours; and the evidence of his intimate, inviolable union with an organised and united Irish nation will make easier and swifter the triumph which in God's providence awaits us.—Yours,

AN IRISH CATHOLIC LAYMAN.

---

* It is hardly necessary to name Cardinals Newman and Manning.

† December 11th.

POSTSCRIPT.

SEVERAL points touched in the foregoing letters require explanation.

1. As to the title "Castle Bishop," this so exactly describes the personage in question that in spite of various criticisms I find myself unable to invent a better. Now, bishops there are in Ireland who have never been to the Castle, nor, as far as the public know, have had any communication therewith, who do its work as thoroughly as if they were its constant attendants, and drew a handsome revenue for their services. Again, there are bishops who have been to the Castle in bodily presence who hate it with an absolute hatred, and who are Irish in every throb of their hearts and every fibre of their brain.

2. "Coming to terms with modern civilisation" has been more than once referred to as practical apostasy, or at least as leading to it. To prevent misconception, it is necessary to define all civilisation as the union of men in society for the mutual aid and the development of the arts of life. Civilisation in the natural order is that which makes itself its own end. Civilisation in the supernatural or Christian order is that which has an end above and beyond itself. In the particular we know that the man who seeks himself his own interest, pleasure, enjoyment—even though the pursuit be regulated by reason and outward decorum—finds himself, indeed, but finds his own ruin. For the supernatural is the complement, and perfection of the natural, wanting which the latter sinks to inevitable decay. Again, the man whose secret aim, desire, object is the supernatural, in apparent neglect of all the world holds dear, finds that which even the world prizes—happiness—and finds also his own higher good—the *summum bonum* of human existence. The civilisation of which each of these men is the type, follows the individual fate for good or evil. Now, it must be granted that English civilisation—and Irish as far as it is West British—is of the natural or pagan kind; and the Catholic ecclesiastic who makes himself one with it, who tolerates it, *who does not fight against it*, as far as his action or inaction goes—involves the Church of God in the ruin which, from the operation of constant necessary laws, sooner or later overtakes such civilisation. While, therefore, we may thankfully take advantage of all the material progress of which the age boasts so much, we must keep steadily in view that it makes no part whatever of that true civilisation which aims at restoring human society, as far as it is possible, to its primal condition.

3. It has been said: How can you, an ultra of the Ultramontanes, support so unreservedly the leadership of a non-Catholic? Some of our friends on the other side, and others at this, openly and secretly point it out as a weakness that we give Mr. Parnell our entire confidence. This

is sufficiently offensive from men of a class who profess Catholicism for no nobler purpose than to enhance their price. Nevertheless, it suggests the usefulness of an explanation which can be readily given.

In addition to being offensive, the insinuation is historically false; for, with few exceptions, the best Irishmen for the last hundred years have been non-Catholics. Beginning with Grattan, Ireland owes more to them than to any others save one. Perhaps the most beautiful character who during the whole period adorned Irish life was the late John Martin. The instinct of the Irish people is more exact than the bastard theology of the purists who would confine the noblest of natural virtues—that one which, in a manner, combines them all—patriotism—to the profession of any class or creed.

There is in all society, whether Christian or pagan, an inherent right to pursue its own lawful ends by its own means. In seeking to re-establish the prosperity of their country by the enaction of laws for the protection of industry, and by gaining power to manage their own affairs, the Irish people are perfectly justified in electing as their chief the man who seems to them most likely to lead them to success, no matter what, in the religious order, he may or may not profess. It is a question of expediency, of means to end, and so likewise is the assistance which the leader may ask or accept. If any political chief were to require a condition of moral perfection in all his followers, he would, if he could begin any movement at all, quickly find himself a general without an army. Supposing, by the favour of Mr. Gladstone, the beastliest form of infidelity, in the person of Mr. Bradlaugh, had got entrance into the House of Commons, Mr. Parnell, while declining to admit him into the Irish party on account of the odium he would attach to it, would be perfectly free to take advantage of his vote on a critical division.

But our choice may be justified on still higher grounds. The charity of the Catholic Church is as wide as that of her Divine Founder. Her solicitude embraces every creature formed in his image. Her jurisdiction extends to every soul on whom the Christian character has been impressed by true baptism. She tells them they are bound to hear her voice and to regard her as their true mother. Declaring with precision the law of which she is the depositary, guardian, and teacher, she is intolerant of its contraries, because she is certain of its truth. She has, in delivering this message, more than the certainty of the exact sciences; for, fully satisfying the most rigorous demands of reason as to her authority, she gives to her subjects the higher, the absolute certainty of faith.

Yet while declaring her message to all men she refrains from judging individuals without her obedience—nor, indeed, does she decide on the condition of those within, save in the rare cases when she raises a saint to her altars or strikes an obdurate sinner with the major excommunication. On the contrary, she permits us to hope that many apparently beyond her pale are in reality her children, born to her in baptism, in good faith obeying conscience, and responding to the grace of the Holy Spirit, "which bloweth where it listeth," in ways not known to men— perhaps approaching the one fold in which, following the general law, God wills all men to be. In that wonderful book, the "Apologia" of Cardinal Newman, we have a forcible example of this truth in his declaration that after he had received (conditional) Catholic baptism his faith was no stronger nor wider than before, which is, by implication, the assurance that he already possessed the fulness of Catholic belief.

4. Here the writer may fitly declare a truth which to him has always been matter of thankfulness—that between English and Irish Protestantism (using the word in its widest sense) there is, in a manner, almost as great a difference as between the general spiritual condition of the two peoples. The Irish Protestant is a far higher type, both in belief and conduct. The difference appears chiefly in the South and West. But truth compels me to except Belfast from this favourable view. It is nearly, if not altogether, as unbelieving and immoral—in its Protestant element—as any Scotch or English town of like size. Whether owing to the purer atmosphere, the higher standard set by the Church, or to inherent merit, we meet in Ireland, not unfrequently, men to whom we may safely extend the charity of the Church, and believe that they are sincere and faithful Christians though not dwelling apparently within her pale.

Passing from this, the writer has the best reason to know that the late Isaac Butt, though, unhappily, not a Catholic, was in sentiment profoundly Christian. He had penetrated the secret of the national life, and drew from his early home that feeling of sympathy with the people and respect for their religious convictions, which led him, at the close of his career, to put himself at their head and inaugurate the movement which has had in other hands such wonderful success. With perfect consistency, therefore, with an entire and unreserved confidence, may the Catholic people of Ireland follow their gallant Protestant chief, not judging him in the spiritual order, but mayhap praying that in God's good time every possible reward may be given him for services and self-sacrifice without parallel in our time. Certain it is that there is incomparably more of the true Christian spirit in the heroic devotion of Parnell to the people and cause with which Catholicism is inseparably linked, than in the piety of the most Catholic Whig lawyer who ever sold himself body and soul to do the diabolical

work of the British Government in Ireland. In the new order so rapidly
being formed out of the ruins of the old there will be in public life no
distinction of Catholic or Protestant, no ascendency, no Pale. Good
citizenship will form the sole title to honour and command ; and, speaking in the name of a people I know well, and in my own, the Catholics
of Ireland do not desire, and would not accept, any condition of things
in which other ideas should prevail.

5. " But," asks a friend, venerable by reason of years and office, still
more venerable from services, "are you quite sure of your ground?
Granting the truth of every word you have written, are you not doing
more evil than good? Are not these letters, after all, rather the outcome
of an idiosyncrasy idealising an ordinary condition of things than a sober
statement of facts as they are? Are you not by externating thoughts
floating in the minds of many, by giving body and form to the inchoate
and intangible, inducing the very evils you desire to prevent, and hastening the final catastrophe when the abomination of desolation shall sit in
the holy place?" I listen to my friend with the more respect because I
am unable to accept his view. It seems tinged with the foreboding
which comes of years and sorrows—sorrows not personal, but for a
desolated country and a suffering people. I ask myself, is the Government
of to-day, less than the Government of last year or last century, a
Government of fraud and force, of chicane and hypocrisy? Are not its
final sanctions, as of old, the bludgeon, the bayonet, and the gibbet? Do
not three of the four crimes calling to heaven for vengeance—wilful
murder, oppression of the poor, and defrauding labourers of their wages—
ravage the land? And do not Catholic ecclesiastics, having power to
stop them, not only sit down and make no sign, but enter into friendly
relations with the criminals?

6. Then, turning once more to the Propaganda Circular, we find
clearest evidences of a condition of mind, of a current of opinion, boding
imminent danger to Ireland and the Church. The Quarantotti Rescript,
while bartering our ecclesiastical freedom for some unknown but un-Irish
equivalent, was at least polite in its terms. The Propaganda Secretary
of to-day, abandoning the stately and elaborate forms of Roman courtesy,
designates our chief, " Parnellius," as he would an unprincipled adventurer, a mercenary agitator, as something at once dangerous and
contemptible; and the nine bishops who had already approved the Tribute,
the thousands of clergy of the second rank, and the whole Irish people,
as " asseclæ "—lacqueys, sycophants, hangers-on ! The scribe who drew
the circular may have been ignorant of what he was doing. The
eminent ecclesiastics who signed it were or were not. If the former, they
showed how matters of infinite importance can be done with unheard-of

carlessness; if the latter, they have put an unparalleled affront on the most loyal and faithful people committed to their care. Again, in the Soderini pamphlet, "published by authority," and in Maziere Brady's "Rome and Fenianism" (written in Rome), a rehash of the vile stuff of the anti-Catholic Dublin press, there is further proof of depth of anti-Irish prejudice in the surroundings of Propaganda.

7. We suffer an unknown detriment from want of University education. We can never reconstitute ourselves thoroughly without it. The three years of University life are what temper and polish the student and make the man. In these he digests and assimilates the acquisitions of college life, and matches himself with his future competitors. It is the attrition of mind with mind in the University, the emulation bred of constant struggles, the training of historical and debating societies, which give the first stimulus to manly effort, the first inception of laudable ambition to succeed in life. As well pit a raw recruit against the veteran of many campaigns as match our youth, half-formed from their college course, against the trained minds of the University. It is unjust, and we will no longer bear injustice; for we do not need. For every man of Irish birth we demand equality before the law. No true Irishman will ever, on Irish soil, ask for more. He would not be worthy of the name if he was content with less. When, therefore, the most eminent ecclesiastic in Ireland comes to us associated with the chief of the anti-Christian sect of Freemasons and of the Orange ascendency faction, red with the blood of our brothers in Derry—when, I say, Cardinal McCabe and the Duke of Abercorn offer us a thrice-condemned Godless examining board, which they call a Royal University, surely it is time to make a stand, surely it is time to say, "Your Eminence, we cannot accept this thing; it is not Catholic nor Irish. It involves the violation of our educational rights, and implies the abandonment of Catholic principles. We therefore reject and abhor it, with the whole train of compromises of which it is the fitting conclusion."

Once for all, we will level up or level down. If a Catholic Trinity be not founded, with equal rights and proportionate endowments, then the Trinity of ascendency must go. We have at length got a foothold on the soil of Ireland. Out of that must come everything we can claim of equality and justice—we will not have fastened upon us, by educational disability, an ascendency more subtle and more potent than any law could invent or impose. For thirty years Ireland has seen her highest interests bartered and juggled away for promotion for the basest of mankind—Whig-Catholic lawyers. She was indignant and outraged, but dumb. What has she gained by quiescence? The Propaganda Circular, and the gagging of every Irish ecclesiastic worthy of the name.

The anti-Irish, anti-Catholic conspiracy grows and gains upon us.

The assembly best representing everything of honesty and loyalty and worth in Ireland met in the Rotunda a few weeks since. Many eloquent voices were heard, but that sacred voice was silent which so long sustained and guided the Irish cause. Again the Irish Church was severed from the Irish people. The Cardinal scored another triumph. He will find a few more such victories fatal as those of Pyrrhus.

So much in answer to my venerable friend. One more precaution against the evils he dreads. I beg my readers to keep always in view the distinctions made in an earlier letter. Whatever the merit or demerit of ecclesiastics, the Church is not touched in her Divine life. That always remains perfect and immaculate. If it were otherwise, our Lord could not dwell within her. She retains through all vicissitudes the same absolute indefeasible claim to our obedience and love, because in her totality she remains perfect, and everywhere possesses and guards the Life of our life. When, therefore, faithful Catholics see anything in the clergy to give them pain, they should draw closer to their Mother because some of her sons may act unworthily. This is where true loyalty is shown, and faith and constancy are tried.

8. For those who have followed me so far with sympathy and indulgence in dealing in a manner necessarily very imperfect with a difficult and complicated subject, no further profession of faith is necessary. For those, again (and I hope they are few), who consider these letters hostile criticism from without—instead of what they really are, filial remonstrances from within—no words of mine could give them a contrary impression. For those whose opinions may be yet undecided, I will repeat that as for myself I could choose no higher good than to be faithful to death for what is to be prized above life itself, so for Ireland I can desire no less. Sooner would I see the last man of Irish race perish than that one ray of her sole but incomparable glory—her fidelity to the Catholic faith and the See of Peter—should be dimmed or withdrawn. For myself, I have the most profound conviction that, in spite of so much to endanger and disquiet us, Ireland is destined to remain, and to become still more, the most Catholic of nations. Her glorious apostle did not pray for three years on the mount which bears his name without effect. More certain hope than even this : we rest upon . the Rock ; we look with calm and perfect confidence to the chair of Peter, and know with absolute certainty that the voice which will issue therefrom when the cause is finally judged will be the voice of the Holy Spirit. In due time the prelates who possess the confidence and who command the obedience of the Irish people will put before the Holy Father the truth

and justice of our cause, and by this statement our adversaries will be confuted and confounded. It could not be otherwise, for we are Catholic before all. It is, in truth, impossible for those whose souls have once embraced the Christian idea, who give themselves lovingly to its consideration, who know the serenity and elevation of mind it brings, or sometimes, coming unawares, how it floods the soul with sweetness and light—it is impossible that they can ever turn away from the absolutely True and Good at the instance of human passion or ambition, for what is, at best, indifferent—at worst, corrupt. There is no correlation between things different in kind. Neither can we compare the finite with the infinite—time with eternity. Perpetual youth, a million of worlds, an eternity of their enjoyment, all the pleasures of sense and intellect, are to the soul which has once tasted the ineffable sweetness of Divine wisdom not of a moment's consideration, not of a feather's weight, against that one absorbing, consuming thought, that ray of Divine light, that relation of origin and congruity which binds her to her God. This advantage, this benefit, this priceless heritage, this blessing beyond compare, comes to us and remains with us because of our inviolable union with Rome, and this union we will guard and maintain while a man of Irish name remains on Irish soil.

The words of a great man, still living, adorn the first page of this book. With those of another, gone to his reward, it may, I trust, be fitly closed. They form part of the 39th Conference of Lacordaire; and even in their clumsy English dress read like that grandest outcome of Inspiration, " *In principio erat Verbum:* " " There is a man over Whose tomb love still keeps guard. There is a Man Whose sepulchre is not only glorious, as was predicted by the prophet, but even beloved. There is a Man Whose ashes after eighteen centuries have not yet grown cold, Who is every day born anew in the memory of countless multitudes; Who is visited in his tomb by shepherds and by kings, who vie with one another in offering Him their homage. There is a man whose steps are continually being tracked, and Who, withdrawn as He is from our bodily eyes, is still discerned by those who unweariedly haunt the spots were once He suffered, and who seek Him on His Mother's knees by the border of the lake, on the mountain top, in the secret paths of the valleys, under the shadow of the olive trees, or in the silence of the desert. There is a Man Who has died and been buried, but Whose sleeping and waking is still watched by us— Whose every word still vibrates in our hearts, producing there something more than love, for it gives life to those virtues of which love is the mother. There is a Man Who long ages ago was fastened to a gibbet. And that Man is every day taken down from the throne of His passion by millions of adorers, who prostrate themselves on the earth before Him, and kiss his bleeding feet with unspeakable emotion.   There is a Man Who was once scourged and slain and crucified, but Whom an ineffable passion. has raised from death and infamy, and made the object of an unfailing love which finds all in Him peace, honour, joy—nay, even ecstasy There is a Man Who, pursued to death in His own time with inextinguishable hate, has demanded apostles and martyrs from each successive generation, and has never failed to find them.   There is one Man, and one alone, Who has established this love on earth, and it is Thou, O my Jesus!—Thou Who has been pleased to anoint, to consecrate me in thy love, and Whose very name at this moment suffices to move my whole being, and to tear from me those words in spite of myself."

APPENDIX.

For the convenience of the reader, the authorised translation of the Circular of Propaganda is added, with the articles from the *Nation*, which they drew forth. These latter have a permanent value, which make them worthy of being rescued—as far as this place may do so—from the oblivion which attends on newspaper literature. They have never been answered, for the best of all reasons.

LETTER OF THE SACRED CONGREGATION DE PROPAGANDA FIDE TO THE BISHOPS OF IRELAND.

ILLUSTRIOUS AND REVEREND LORD,—

Whatever may be the opinion formed as to Mr. Parnell himself and his objects, it is at all events proved that many of his followers have on many occasions adopted a line of conduct in open contradiction to the rules laid down by the Supreme Pontiff in his letter to the Cardinal Archbishop of Dublin, and contained in the instructions sent to the Irish Bishops by this Sacred Congregation, and unanimously accepted by them at their recent meeting at Dublin. It is true that according to those instructions *it is lawful for the Irish to seek redress for their grievances and to strive for their rights ;* but always at the same time observing the Divine maxim *to seek first the kingdom of God and His justice;* and remembering also *that it is wicked to further any cause, no matter how just, by unlawful means.*

It is, therefore, the duty of all the clergy, *and especially of the Bishops, to curb the excited feelings of the multitude, and to take every opportunity, with timely exhortations, to recall them to the justice and moderation which are necessary in all things, that so they may not be led by greed of gain to form a wrong estimate of their true interests, or to place their hopes of public prosperity in the shame of criminal acts.* Hence it follows that it is not permitted to any of the clergy to depart from these rules themselves, or to take part in, or in any way promote, movements inconsistent with prudence and with the duty of calming men's minds.

It is certainly not forbidden to contribute money for the relief of distress in Ireland ; but at the same time the aforesaid Apostolic mandates absolutely condemn such collections as are got up in order to inflame popular passions, and to be used as the means for leading men into rebellion against the laws. Above all things, such collections should be avoided where it is plain that hatred and dissensions are aroused by them, that distinguished persons are loaded with insults, that never in any way are censures pronounced against the crimes and murders with which wicked men stain themselves; and especially when it is asserted that the measure of true patriotism is in proportion to the amount of money given or refused, so as to bring the people under the pressure of intimidation.

In these circumstances, it must be evident to your Lordship, that the collection called the "*Parnell Testimonial Fund*" cannot be approved by this Sacred Congregation; and consequently it cannot be tolerated that any ecclesiastic, much less a Bishop, should take any part whatever in recommending or promoting it.

Meanwhile, I pray God long to preserve your Lordship.

Given from the palace of the Sacred Congregation de Propaganda Fide 11th day of May, 1883.

JOHN CARDINAL SIMEONI, *Prefect.*
DOMINICK, ARCHBISHOP OF TYRE, *Secretary.*

NOTE.—This translation is not exact.

THE ROMAN LETTER.

(From the "Nation" of May 19th, 1883.)

THERE is evil and disastrous news from Rome. Never since the priceless treasure of the Faith was brought to our Irish shore has so terrible a stroke been dealt at religion in Ireland as it is our lot to chronicle to-day.

The deadly intrigues of England have triumphed at the Propaganda. The sword is drawn on our faithful and devoted prelates and priests.

May the God of our fathers be with Ireland in this cruel moment! Now, indeed, must we show that our fidelity to religion and our historic devotion to the Holy See can come scathless through an ordeal more trying than the blazing faggots of Elizabeth or the merciless massacres of Cromwell.

As we have through blood and fire held our Faith against England, so shall we at all human price hold our country against Rome. We will not desert our priests and prelates; they will not desert us. If force, spiritual or temporal, come to tear them and us asunder, we will call to mind ere now those who in an evil moment were enabled to speak in the name of the Supreme Pontiff were (fortunately for Rome and for Ireland) resisted—and successfully resisted—by O'Connell, with Catholic Ireland at his back.

A letter has been addressed by the Propaganda to our Irish prelates, in which the inconceivable outrage is offered to our country of mixing up crimes and disorders wholly abominable, and detested by all good Catholics and good citizens, with the justifiable and legitimate political warfare waged by the Irish people for the defence of their lives and the recovery of their just rights. Long has England tried to get the world to do what the Propaganda has herein at last done—that is to say, to class together, as of one and the same moral character, the lawful resistance of the Irish people to oppression, illegality, fraud, and destruction, and the execrable disorders (really the evil products and outgrowths of that oppression and illegality) which unhappily may attend upon acute stages of popular exasperation.

What can the Propaganda say—what could be suggested by the British spy who for the past sixteen months has been traducing us and our prelates and priests in secret at Rome, in denunciation of crime that has not been a thousand-fold more strongly said on countless occasions by ourselves and by those priests and prelates? It shall not be said, for it cannot be said, that Catholic Ireland has so changed as to resent a reprehension of crime from a tribunal of God's Church. No, no, Monsignori; not so. Your offence against Ireland is that you have espoused the ancient and persistent calumny of our oppressors, in dragging in a proscription of legitimate patriotism within the sweep of a rightful condemnation of crime.

If England's word is to be held good at Rome on such a subject, let us face the consequence. Terrible were the crimes, frightful the disorders, during Ireland's hapless condition in the eighteenth century. The bloody atrocities of the law went often side by side with the ruthless barbarities of the "Tory" and the "Rapparee." England called aloud upon the world to execrate the wretches who were resisting her laws; and the Irishman who sheltered a priest or who shot down a trooper—the peasant who stole to mass on a Sunday or the peasant who fired the Williamite usurper's mansion—were "tarred with the same brush." Nay, indeed, the records of the period show us that, *then as now*, the priests and the laymen who were most innocent of complicity in disorder were foully declared to be the "real" authors of all crime; while the people, because they would not love and obey the law, and give up alike the priest and the murderer, were declared to be "sympathisers with assassination."

All the way right down through our history comes the same abominable effort of England to classify Irish patriotism with Irish crime.

Take the period of the Tithe War :—

Even apart from the scenes of bloodshed actually incidental to the struggle against tithes, agrarian outrage rose to a terrible pitch. Every circuit had its "bloody assize." Forth from the press of England—from the statesmen, the legislators, the agents

(open and secret, ecclesiastical and lay) of England—there burst
a continuous roar of defamation, in which O'Connell and the
Irish priesthood were held up as the secret inciters and real
authors of Irish murder, turbulence, and crime. *Then, as to-day,* every
passionate sentence that could be culled, *longo intervallo,* from hundreds
of speeches—every hasty word, amidst thousands spoken in restraint
and noble exhortation to tranquillity and peace—every regrettable act of
omission or commission in the heat and turmoil of a desperate conflict
in a cause righteous before God—was patched and pieced together so as
to startle one with an apparent unity and continuity. "Behold !" cried
England, "behold the language and the deeds of these Irish demagogues,
priests and laymen. Why does not the Pope denounce them ?"

Nor was it only O'Connell and his lay associates whom England,
according to her traditional custom of moral assassination, held up as
accountable for Irish crime. *Then, as now,* Irish priests *by name,* Irish
prelates *by name,* were denounced to the Pope (in secret) by paid emissaries of the English Government. The late ever-lamented illustrious
Archbishop of our Great Western Diocese was able to exhibit proofs of a
startling episode in the history of English secret intrigues with Rome.
Vehement efforts were secretly made by the English Government to
prevent his elevation to the See of St. Jarlath. Lay "Catholics" were
sent to Rome to stab his character ; and

> *He was confronted with a collection or compilation of "inflammatory"
> speeches or letters to the press alleged to have been made or written
> by him or his associates and friends in Irish politics, as tending
> to show complicity in or encouragement of lawlessness, outrage, and
> crime !*

That compilation was an elaborate task. Who did it ? Who had the
newspaper files searched through ? Who sent a British "Catholic" spy
to Rome with the deadly indictment in his bag ?

The English Minister of *that* day simply did what the English
Minister of *to-day* has done. But in *that* day it was done in vain.
To-day it has succeeded !

And the Propaganda talks to us of "prudence" and "wisdom,"
forsooth ! In these temporal affairs we Irishmen have shown ourselves
better stewards than the disastrous counsellors of the Holy Father have
been. For while we, who succeeded to a national inheritance, as it were,
only *in esse,* have, step by step, been recovering and winning the ancient
possessions and rights, prerogatives and influences, of our nation, their
Eminences of Rome have been losing to the Holy See, piecemeal, all its
territory, all its peoples, all its temporal rights, all its temporal
possessions. So "wisely" and so "prudently" have they managed those

things, that we faithful Catholics have to-day to see in grief and shame the Venerable Father of Christendom, whose power once filled, and ought still to fill, the civilised world, reduced to temporal helplessness and insignificance!

One possession there yet remained which *unwisdom* and *imprudence* could alienate for a moment from the Holy See. One country—and we might almost say *only* one, were it not for our suffering-sister nation, Poland—there yet remained where in the hearts of the people and in the national spirit there mingled fidelity to the Holy See and devotion to Fatherland. In "Catholic" Italy the Pope may be robbed; in "Catholic" Portugal nuns insulted in the public street; in "Catholic" Austria a Concordat trampled under foot; in "Catholic" France religion openly dethroned by popular vote; in "Catholic" Spain the popular heart also lost to or estranged from the Church. But in Ireland as in Poland there yet remained unshaken an indissoluble love of God and love of country. For God and for country we to-day invoke all Catholic Irishmen to confront, in a spirit worthy of religious men and patriotic citizens, the attempts to reduce Irish Catholics to the condition of those Continental peoples who, first separated from their pastors, soon unhappily found other and less worthy guides, and ere long marched on to infidelity with the cry of "No Priests in Politics!"

Prudence, true prudence, must be our care just now, equally with firmness and determination. We will hold fast our faith, no matter what may be the temptations or the provocations to which we may be subjected; but as for our country, on no account whatsoever shall we surrender or abandon its sacred cause. If Rome will enter into an unholy alliance with England against us, then, trusting in the help of the good God, we shall stand for the national rights and liberties of Ireland against Rome and England.

"THE VETO."

From the "Nation" of May 26th, 1883.)

THE many references made just now to "the Veto" and to O'Connell's great triumph on that question suggests the desirability of briefly recalling the exact facts of the Veto contest, and particularly of the Liberator's share in that memorable struggle. In outline, doubtless, the truth on the subject is generally known even amongst other than educated persons; but there is reason to doubt even if all fairly educated Irishmen are acquainted with the details. The importance of the story need not be pointed out, and the lessons taught by its perusal concerns not only Irish Catholics but also the British Government and the Holy See.

K

The, more recent agitation of the Catholic question may be said to have commenced in this century in the year 1805. The commencement was feeble and hesitating, for the political troubles and the Government barbarities of the few preceding years had wellnigh crushed all hope of a better future in the minds both of the people and of their leaders. In one respect, however, matters had improved since 1799, when the Irish bishops, or at least some of them, frightened by the terrible condition in which they found themselves, passed a formal resolution accepting the principle of British control in the appointment of the members of their own body. In the year 1808 they practically rescinded that resolution, and declared against any such concession as was involved in it being given to England in return for a measure of Catholic Emancipation. This was a blow to the hopes of the English, who would at any time after 1800 have thought " emancipation with securities " a good bargain, and with whom, of course, the notion of such a settlement originated. But they did not abandon the scheme of getting control over the Irish Catholic Church, and thereby a political power in Ireland which they could never otherwise have obtained. Three different sets of circumstances favoured their aims : First, a section of the Irish Catholics—mostly aristocrats who merely cared for the privileges they would personally acquire from emancipation, and place-hunters like Richard Lalor Shiel—expressed themselves willing to give " securities " to the Government. Secondly, the English Catholics, including the English Catholic bishops, with one notable exception, took the same side. Thirdly, the Holy See was just then contending with England's great enemy—Napoleon—and, consequently, was much tempted to do England what service it could in the hope of receiving aid in return against the great despot of the Continent. How England strove at Rome to gain her ends is told in many books ; but perhaps the following passage, from a biography of Archbishop Murray, by the late venerated Dean Meagher of Dublin—a passage that, with the change of a name or two, might well be written of certain doings at the present time—is as succinct and accurate an account of the matter as any other :—

" A Vetoistical faction in Rome, composed of Irish and English, had already poisoned the public mind, and produced unfavourable impressions, even on many of the Cardinals, by the circulation of the most unfounded misrepresentations ; the calumnies of Sir John Cox Hippesley and other political dabblers in ecclesiastical affairs formed no inconsiderable part of the machinery, while the whole framework of the system was artfully kept together by the powerful intrigues of the British Cabinet. These attempts to intimidate the delegates, although defeated, were nevertheless renewed through the assistance which at this time they had obtained from the Veto-istical portion of the Irish press. Among other publications, some numbers of Carrick's *Morning Post* had been transmitted to Rome, containing a furious paragraph in which the delegation and remonstrance of the laity had been called in question, and repre-senting both as emanating not from the nation but from an unauthorised junta of a few turbulent, hot-headed individuals in Dublin."

Under these circumstances it is not, perhaps, very surprising that, on the 3rd May, 1814, the following announcement appeared in an English paper: "We have just heard from unquestionable authority that the first act of the Pope, on his re-establishment at Rome, was to pass in full consistory—with the Cardinals unanimously agreeing — an arrangement giving to the British Crown the desired security respecting the nomination of Catholic bishops." The news fell like a thunderbolt on Ireland; the mass of the people, lay and clerical, refused to believe it. But a few days afterwards all doubts on the point were set at rest by the publication of a letter from Monsignor (afterwards Cardinal) Quarantotti, Prefect of the Sacred Congregation of Propaganda, to Dr. Poynter, head of the English hierarchy, conceding the Veto.

It would be impossible to exaggerate the feelings of wonder and alarm which the Quarantotti rescript aroused in Ireland. It scandalised, astounded, and horrified bishops, priests, and people—the weak-kneed and corrupt little faction of Catholics to which we have already referred excepted— for it was seen to be a deadly stroke both to religion and nationality. "An Irish Priest," writing to the *Dublin Evening Post* of the feeling in Dublin said :—

"The ferment spread like wildfire through every gradation of society; and the very lowest order of the people felt its influence. Some cursed, others moaned, all complained. Early this morning my old servant maid, without waiting for any commands of mine, accosted me abruptly with these words: 'Oh ! sir, what shall we do ! *Is it—can it be true that the Pope has turned Orangeman !*' "

The scenes presented by the various chapels on the occasion of the reading of the rescript were touching in the extreme. "The deep silence," says a writer on this subject, "of the fixed and mourning congregations, huddled together in their poor and dimly-lighted churches, hanging on the lips of the preachers—their only consolation, and conscious that the fate of their children, their country, and their Church depended on the conduct of that priesthood—was such as could never be forgotten." Nor did the bishops and the clergy fail to speak out at once the thoughts with which their souls were filled. The letter of the "Irish Priest" already quoted concluded with somewhat remarkable words. "Every attempt," wrote the reverend gentleman, "to weaken the Catholic Church in Ireland shall in the end prove fruitless; and as long as the shamrock shall adorn our island, so long shall the faith delivered to us by St. Patrick prevail in spite of kings, Parliaments, Orangemen, and Quarantottis." Dr. Coppinger, the venerable Bishop of Cloyne, denounced what he called "Mr. Quarantotti's decree" in scathing language. "In common," he wrote, "with every real friend to the integrity of the Catholic religion in Ireland, I read it with feelings of disgust and in-

dignation." Other bishops followed with similar comments, but the first
body of ecclesiastics to pronounce on the rescript was the clergy of
Dublin. They met on the 12th of May, in Bridge Street Chapel, and,
headed by Dr. Blake, P.P., afterwards Bishop of Dromore, they then
passed the following amongst other resolutions :—

> " That we consider the document or rescript signed Quarantotti as non-obligatory
> upon the Catholic Church in Ireland, particularly as it wants those authoritative marks
> whereby the mandates of the Holy See are known and recognised, and especially the
> signature of the Holy Father."
> " That we consider the granting to an anti-Catholic Government any power, either
> direct or indirect, with regard to the appointment and nomination of Catholic bishops
> in Ireland, as at all times inexpedient."

Other clerical protests came forth in due course, and, finally, the bishops
held a Synod at Maynooth, on the 25th of May, at which they resolved
that the decree was not mandatory, and appointed two of their number
to go to Rome as a deputation to argue the whole question with the
Pope in their behalf.

The bishops and the clergy, in short, made a noble stand against the
Veto; but if they had stood alone in their opposition there is little doubt
that the result of the fight would have been different from what it
happily was. Nay, it is hardly going too far to say that if the laity,
headed by O'Connell, had not intervened on the side of Ireland and
Catholicity in this country, some of the bishops themselves would
have eventually recalled their *non possumus* and accepted a Veto in one
guise or another. As a matter of fact, after the escript of Quarantotti
had been withdrawn, Dr. Doyle and other prelates were for accepting a
measure of emancipation qualified by the concession to the British
Government of at least some share in the appointment of Irish bishops.
This fact is placed beyond all doubt by many documents, including letters
from Dr. Doyle himself to Sir Henry Parnell—one of the leading
champions of the Catholic cause in Parliament, and grand-uncle, by the
way, of the present Irish leader. But O'Connell, backed by the laity,
did intervene—happily for religion and country—and won the fight. All
through—from 1800 to 1814—he saw clearly the effect of putting the
Irish Church in any degree in the power of the British Government;
and throughout all those years he constantly proclaimed that nothing
but unqualified, unconditional emancipation would be accepted by the
nation. He rejected with scorn all compromises, all projects for giving
to the Crown "securities for the loyalty" of Irish priests or bishops;
and he never ceased pouring out scorn or ridicule on the authors of those
projects—whether they were Irish, or English, or Roman—in language
which would, doubtless, sound exceedingly strange at the present day to
many who revere his memory as the greatest Catholic statesman of the

century. Let us here give, in illustration, a few extracts from his anti-Veto speeches. On the 28th of May, 1813, speaking of the Catholic Relief Bill of that session, he said :—

"I will not ask you as Catholics, but I will boldly demand of you as Irishmen, whether you do not rejoice at having escaped from an Act of Parliament the necessary consequences of which I have thus laid before you ? Do you not rejoice that the corrupt influence of the Government is not to be extended to your Church, and that there remains, and will remain, in Ireland, one spot free from Ministerial pollution, and that your bishops are not to be degraded to the subserviency of gaugers and tide-waiters, nor your priesthood to the dependence of police-constables ? If your feelings and opinions be, as your approbation of these sentiments proclaim them to be, accordant with mine—if you dread as Catholics, and abhor as Irishmen, the extension of the influence of the servants of the Crown—an influence equally fatal to religion and liberty—you will join with all your hearts in the unanimous adoption of my motion."

Speaking in Cork, on the 13th April, 1813, and referring to the aristocratic Catholics of the Local Catholic Board, who had retired from a great public meeting at which O'Connell attended, because the demand there made was for unconditional emancipation, the Liberator said :—

"I saw them a few moments back, a few scattered individuals in a corner of a yard. I addressed them, because though small, very small indeed in their numbers, yet as individuals they are respectable, and I wished to undeceive them in their error. I asked them, if they were Catholics, and could they talk about securities ? I told them to leave securities to the minions of the Castle—to the pensioned hirelings of the State—aye, and to the Orange Papists, too; but let them not as honest, honourable worthy Catholics insult the public ears with so discordant a sound."

In January, 1815, he declared he desired unanimity, "but," he added " I now disclaim it for ever, if it be not to be had without this concession. I will for ever divide with the men who, directly or indirectly, consent to Vetoism of any description." In the same speech he said :—

"If the Veto, if the interference of the Crown with our religion, were a question exclusively religious, I should leave it at once to the bishops. But it is infinitely interesting as a political measure. It is an attempt to acquire without expense an influence greater than any minister could purchase for millions. Who is there that does not feel the vital, the pressing danger to liberty that results from ministerial. influence ? We owe it to ourselves, and to the Protestants equally, to resist this contagious interference; and every duty that can urge a man to a public disclosure of facts, interesting to every class in the State, calls on me to declare that there exists a conspiracy against the religion of the Irish Catholics, and in its effects against the liberties of all the Irish people ! I state it as a fact that a negotiation is going on between Lord William Bentinck, Lord Castlereagh, and Cardinal Gonsalvi, one result of which is intended by the two former to be the concession to the Minister of the Crown of an effectual supremacy over the Catholic Church in Ireland ; and there is every reason to dread that the Cardinal only waits to get what he considers an adequate compensation before he accedes to the measure. . . . Let our determination never to assent reach Rome. It can easily be transmitted there ; but even should it fail I am still determined to resist. I am sincerely a Catholic, but I am not a Papist. I deny the doctrine that the Pope has any temporal authority, directly or indirectly, in Ireland ; we have all denied it on oath, and we would die to resist it."

O'Connell expressed the most entire confidence in the fidelity of the bishops and the clergy, but he did not hesitate to tell them what, in his opinion, would happen should they, even through good intentions, yield

to the designs of the English. He said in the same speech from which
we have made the foregoing quotations :—

"Yes ; as our former prelates met persecution and death without faltering, the
bishops of the present day will triumph over the treachery of base-minded Catholics
and insidious Ministers of Government. But even should any of our prelates fail,
there is still resource. It is to be found in the unalterable constancy of the Catholic
people of Ireland. If the present clergy shall descend from the high station they
hold, to become the vile slaves of the clerks of the Castle—a thing I believe
impossible—but should it occur, I warn them in time to look to their masters for
their support ; for the people will despise them too much to contribute."

On the point of Roman interference in Irish political affairs O'Connell was
particularly outspoken. "We now exhibit the determination," he said on
the 29th August, 1815, "which we have always avowed, to resist any
measures originating in Rome of a political tendency or aspect. I know
of no foreign prince whom, in temporal matters, the Catholics would
more decidedly resist than the Pope ; and this while they respected and
recognised his spiritual authority." Animadverting on another occasion
on what he termed "the attempt made by the slaves of Rome to instruct
the Irish Roman Catholics upon the manner of their emancipation," he
said : "I would as soon receive my politics from Constantinople as from
Rome !" As for Quarantotti, he met with very scant courtesy indeed
from the Irish leader. "How dare," said the latter, on the 19th May,
1814, in Stephen's Green, "how dare Quarantotti dictate to the people
of Ireland?" The nation roused itself under the spell of the patriot-
orator's words, and although coercion by Dublin Castle was employed to
help forward the Veto project—the Catholic Board, for instance, having
been proclaimed pretty much as the Land League was a year and a half
since—nevertheless the public voice was heard in thundrous accents on
the burning question of the hour. Take the following resolution, which
was passed at the great meeting at Stephen's Green, to which we have
just referred :—

"Resolved—That we deem it a duty to ourselves and our country solemnly and
distinctly to declare that any decree, mandate, or decision whatsoever of any foreign
power or authority, religious or civil, ought not, and cannot of right, assume any
dominion or control over the political concerns of the Catholics of Ireland."

Little more remains to be told. For a short time the Veto rescript
remained in force, but only for a short time. Condemned by the all but
united voice of Ireland, it was at length withdrawn, and its author was
at the same time removed from his post. Did space permit, there are
many reflections which might be made on this scheme to bind the
Catholic Church in Ireland in British fetters, and on the manner in
which it was defeated. It is scarcely necessary, however, that we should
point the moral of the tale. That moral is obvious in every line, and it
is as important as it is obvious.

THE VETO AND THE CIRCULAR.

(From the "Nation" of June 2, 1883.)

NOTWITHSTANDING the painful nature of the outrage offered to Ireland in the Propaganda Letter, it was our conviction from the very first that any danger to the interests of religion which might ensue would be caused less by the angry reclamations of the Irish people than by the language of the Errington-Simeoni party. Our anticipations were well founded, and already deplorable mischief looms on the horizon.

The line adopted is one, the evil tendencies of which can be seen at a glance. It is contended that the Letter is all the Pope's own idea ; that Mr. Errington has had nothing whatever to do with it : that Lord Granville has had no hand whatever in it ; that the Pope has been neither misinformed nor insufficiently informed ; that " both sides " and all sides were fully heard by the Pope ; that he knows better than Irishmen do what goes on in Ireland ; that he knows better than Irishmen do what they think in their own minds, or mean or intend in subscribing to the Parnell Fund ; that the Pope having declared that they design and intend it as a help to violence and crime, they *do* so design and intend it, though they themselves may not be aware of the fact ; that they, therefore, must not subscribe to the Parnell Fund, no matter from what good or pure or noble motive, since the Pope knows their motives best ; that for anyone to say the alleged facts and circumstances on which the Pope's Letter is based are non-existent, and that the Propaganda Letter ought to be recalled, is defying Peter and resisting the voice of the Church.

Now, there is no more pernicious mode of weakening or destroying the authority of the Holy See, to which we Catholic Irishmen have ever been faithful, than by this style of language. For if what is just now being written in Vatican journals in Rome and England be true, the instantaneous, the loud, angry, and indignant protests of the bishops, priests, and people of Ireland against the Rescript of Pope Pius VII., establishing the Veto, were wicked and rebellious, defiance of Peter, and resistance of the voice of the Church.

We put it to the conscience and judgment of any man of calm and sober mind within the pale of the Catholic Church : Is it a good thing for religion, is it conducive to confidence in the Holy See, that the Irish people—knowing all they know about the Veto ; knowing all they know about British intrigue with Cardinal Quarantotti ; knowing all they know of the part borne by English Catholics in that transaction ; knowing as they know that *that* stroke at their liberties (averted by the stern resistance of the Irish people) was as truly and fully a Papal act as is this recent letter from the Propaganda—should be told the choice before them is submission to or severance from Rome?

Evil is the hour in which this baleful idea is thrust forward. There is nothing more fatal to authority than subjecting it unnecessarily to strain, especially strain that may prove to be too severe. It is mischief pure and simple to be familiarising the popular mind with such an alternative as "submission or revolt," solely for the purpose of buttressing up a dubious transaction. We quite agree with the contention that the figure of speech, or the resort, of appealing "from the Pope ill-informed to the Pope well-informed" is one that might be used as an excuse by the veriest schismatic or heretic; but the real question is whether it may not, on the other hand, be also used in wisdom and good faith, for a very salutary purpose, by the best friends and truest counsellors of the Holy See. That is to say, it may be used to avert collision, it may be used to save authority from discredit or injury. When Pope Clement so far harked in with the anti-Jesuit crusade, in presence of a howl raised by all the infidels and tyrants of Europe, as to decree the suppression of the heroic Society of Jesus—when Pope Pius the Seventh was so far "misled" or "misinformed" as to concede the Veto in 1814—it was wiser to say, "This act will be reconsidered; the Pope has been misinformed;" or to say, as is said, in effect—and, indeed, almost in terms—by an English Catholic journal, "even in such cases the Pope is right; he can never be misinformed; the Veto was right; the suppression of the Jesuits was right; the English Government ought to have a voice in the selection of Irish bishops; the Jesuits ought to be suppressed; the Pope knows best on all these points; he is never ill-informed; the Vicar of Christ stands on a higher ground than all the Governments of the world, and his judgments are pronounced in a serener atmosphere"—and so the Jesuits should have been kept down, and the Veto kept up.

Who is the best friend of religion, who is the wisest counsellor of Rome—the man who seeks to link the Pope's spiritual authority irrevocably to acts that, as a matter of fact, are open to review, and who madly demands that that authority shall sink or swim with them; or he who says, "There is nothing inconsistent with the sacred authority of the Holy See, nothing inconsistent with the unchanged and unchangeable teaching of the Church, nothing inconsistent with the Divine guarantee of infallible teaching, in a Pope recalling an administrative act and restoring the Jesuits, or cancelling the deadly Veto, or withdrawing an undeserving censure on an Irish national movement?"

The point is so simple that it can be grasped alike by the most profound theologian or the humblest peasant in Ireland: Either the Pope

was right or the Pope was wrong on the Veto. If we suppose him to
have been right, how are we to regard the conduct of Daniel O'Connell
and the Irish people? How are we to regard the conduct of the Irish
archbishops, bishops, and priests? Above all, how are we to regard the
conduct of the Pope himself in practically withdrawing his rescript?
Does the *Tablet* wish Irish Catholics to believe that the Pope was right,
that there was no error, that there was no lack of accurate information
and wise counsel, but that the Holy See flinched before "outcry and
insubordination in Ireland?" Is this more true, and is it more edifying,
than our version, namely, that the Holy Father, on further consideration,
on fuller information, and on sounder counsels, withdrew the Veto and
saved religion in Ireland?

We put it straight to the prelates of Ireland—and the point is vital
just now: Is it good for religion, is it a service to the Holy See, that our
people should be asked to believe that the Pope is incapable of error in
political and temporal affairs? Or is it more conducive to the interests
of faith, and is it truer loyalty to the Holy See to maintain that the
Supreme Pontiff deals with facts or alleged facts as they are laid before
him, and may at any moment recall, vary, rescind, or cancel any administrative act, on more mature consideration, and on a more full and
accurate knowledge of the circumstances? This is a subject which
cannot without danger to religion be paltered with at a moment so
critical as the present. The pretence that the letter of Cardinal
Quarantotti in 1814, or the letter of Cardinal Simeoni in 1883, should
not be questioned, discussed, or resisted, any more than the Dogma of
the Trinity, or of the Immaculate Conception, or of the infallibility of
Papal teaching *ex cathedra*, can only lead to one result. For Irish
bishops and Irish priests this is now a pressing question, and we look to
them to give it a reassuring and a satisfactory solution.

FACTS FOR THE PROPAGANDA.

(*From the "Nation" of June 2nd*, 1883.)

THE .British agent at Rome has persuaded the Cardinal Secretary of the
Propaganda that "priests in politics," or the participation of the
Catholic clergy in the civil life of their country, has had an evil effect in
Ireland. He plainly enough tells us that if our prelates had kept their
priests off Land League platforms, and set their faces against Mr. Parnell
and the Irish party, the murder-leagues of the Irish Carbonari would
never have been known.

There are a few matters of fact relating to this view which the
Cardinal Secretary can easily test and verify for himself.

The first is that the Carbonari—the real original fraternity of that ill-omened name, whom we shudder to see any Irishman imitating—are the growth and product of his Eminence's own country, not of ours. Yea, are the growth and product of a "No-Priests-in-Politics" policy wherever, unhappily, they appear.

The second is that wherever the Carbonari, the Illuminati, or any other of those unhallowed secret confederacies have once been able to establish themselves, they wisely recognise that the priest in politics would be fatal to their designs; and so the Carbonari take for *their* motto, "No Priests in Politics."

The third is one well worthy of investigation by the Propaganda. Let all possible inquiry test these all-important and all-convincing facts :

The three murder-leagues that have so startled and horrified us in Ireland have been these, viz. :—

Maamtrasna,
Crossmaglen,
Dublin.

Maamtrasna is in the arch-Diocese of Tuam.
Crossmaglen is in the Archdiocese of Armagh.
Dublin is, of course, in the Archdiocese of Dublin.

The three Irish prelates affected (according to the Propaganda doctrine), therefore, are—

Most Rev. Archbishop McEvilly,
Most Rev. Archbishop McGettigan,
His Eminence Cardinal McCabe.

Is Dr. McEvilly a Land Leaguer? Is Dr. McGettigan? Is Cardinal McCabe? Is it much short of a libel on the Archbishop of Tuam to say he has encouraged Mr. Parnell's movement in any shape or form? Is it much less than a calumny to insinuate of Dr. McGettigan that he has ever forwarded or aided the Land League? What shall we say of Cardinal McCabe in such a connection? Is it not recorded in Downing Street how his Eminence has, from first to last, denounced the movement that saved the Irish people from ruin and brought forth Mr. Gladstone's Land Act of 1881?

The three Archbishops of Ireland who in this whole business have in their several dioceses most vehemently carried out the policy exhorted to us—if not, indeed, commanded—by the Propaganda, are—

Dr. McEvilly,
Dr. McGettigan,
Cardinal McCabe.

And those dioceses have given to us—

> The Maamtrasna Murder League,
> The Crossmaglen Murder League,
> The Dublin Murder League.

Indeed, his Eminence of Dublin can boast of or weep for *two* murder leagues—Mr. Carey's "Invincibles" and Mr. Devine's "Avengers."

"Shun the Land League and stick to the Sodalities" sounds a very pious maxim. Indeed, Cardinal McCabe early wanted our wives and sisters to be banished from the Sodalities if they dared to help the Land League. Well, Mr. James Carey shunned the Land League and was deep in the Sodalities. Will the Cardinal Secretary just inquire who this last-named spiritual subject of Cardinal McCabe's diocese happens to be?

Meantime, what of the *fourth* Archdiocese of Ireland? What have the spiritual subjects of his Grace the Archbishop of Cashel contributed to this bloody business?

Nothing—just nothing!

Yes, Tipperary, once torn and stained by terrible deeds of violence, through these recent years of fierce excitement has presented a spectacle of public peace and practical devotion to religion. In no other part of Ireland have prelate, priests, and people been more united in earnest participation in the national struggle. In no part of Ireland have there been fewer crimes. In no other part of Ireland is religion more an edifying reality at the altar and in the homes of the people.

Nor does Cashel and Emly stand alone in this significant and splendid contrast to Tuam, Armagh, and Dublin.

"He who runs may read." We invite the Propaganda to study the lesson.

NOTE.—The foregoing articles from the *Nation* form nearly the last, as they are amongst the ablest and best, contributed by the late Alex. M. Sullivan to the cause of Faith and Fatherland.

EXTRACT OF LETTER TO COUNT MONTALEMBERT BY G. H. MOORE, LATE M.P. FOR MAYO.

(Referred to in page xiv.)

The *Times*, after introducing you to the intelligent British public as a well-known "defender of the Gallican liberties," instructs them "that your work is destined to be remarkable." It is a noble and passionate eulogy of English freedom, the language of which extraordinary composition is a stream of unpausing eloquence." This

specimen of well-informed criticism and accurate English is at once
adopted by the enlightened body to which it is addressed.   The
" British Christian" bows down to you in reverence as the sworn foe
of "Ultramontanism," which is his present idea of the evil principle,
and the English people generally think it but just to repay your
elaborate flatteries of everything that is English by a vigorous development of all those "ridiculous and offensive exaggerations and gratuitous
insults to foreigners and attempts at interference in the internal affairs
of other countries" which you yourself describe as one of their
exquisite developments of liberty of speech.

Do not suppose that I do not cordially concur in much that you
have said, and in much more that you might have said, of the noble
attributes of the English character.   No man admires more than I do,
no man is more willing to recognise the genius and the virtues, the
great energies and the great deeds of the people of England.   I
respect and appreciate the bravery that has never been surpassed, and
the resolution and perseverance that have rarely been equalled, the
energy that never falters, the industry that never tires, the thrift
that never wastes, and the generosity that never fails.   They have all
the homely energies that make a people great, and almost all the higher
inspirations that make a nation glorious; and when their history is the
history of the past, many and heavy as have been their errors and their
crimes, there is no race among the children of men that will have done
more for the greater interests of mankind than that which is called the
Anglo-Saxon.   But, like the children in the fairy tale, upon whom many
beneficent spirits have conferred their choicest gifts—all marred and
perverted by the curse of one malevolent fairy that was not invited to
the christening—there is one giant vice that poisons at their very source
the energies and the virtues of this great people.

A writer whose words you quote has designated, although indistinctly,
one of the leading features of this their evil genius : "Intolerable
national prejudice and a pride without limit and without prudence, which
is revolting to other nations and dangerous in itself."   This, however, is
not all : it is but a branch of that which is the root of all—a self-worship,
the most inordinate and absorbing and overruling that ever "darkened
the human reason or hardened the human heart," a terrible national
idolatry to which human feelings and human consciences are expected to
bow down in worship, to which all the rights of all other men are offered
up in remorseless sacrifice.   On what point is it that the "intolerable
national prejudice" of which you speak runs riot and the pride exceeds
all limit and all prudence?   Of the vast commerce which shadows every
ocean with its canvas, of the gigantic industry which has made England

the workshop of the world, of the mighty struggles they have maintained in defence of their own liberties, of the efforts they have made to repress slavery and to colonise the world with free men, of all that is good and great in their nature and their history, Englishmen are certainly not over-proud. What other people would bear such large honours with a modesty more decent? It is only on the subject of their gross insular habits, their stupid insular prejudices, their narrow insular opinions, their exceptional insular institutions, their absurd insular religion, that they are arrogant, tyrannical, and cruel. They are firmly persuaded that a body of institutions, civil and religious, which are but the type and embodiment of their own habits, passions, prejudices, and superstitions, are fitted to meet all the exigencies of all the human race, and ought to be forced upon the convictions of every people in the world. "Such a thing as that would never do in England,' means, in the mind of an Englishman, that the institution to which he is pleased to allude is utterly unreasonable, and should be resisted at once by all but idiots and slaves. On the other hand, "such an institution has been found to succeed in England," means, in like manner, that if it has not succeeded among any other people it is owing to some inherent and degrading defect in their organisation, and that in itself it is adapted to supply all human wants, temporal and eternal. The consequence is that while among Englishmen proper, of whose feelings and interests English institutions have been the growth and are the ready instrument, these institutions have been loved and successful; all other nations who have felt their operation have either shaken them off as intolerable or regarded them as the engines of fraud and oppression. And this not because Englishmen are naturally unjust or indisposed to mercy; but because they will persist in endeavouring to generate out of a hybrid and sterile egotism that social vigour and patriotic life which can only be begotten by the genial instincts and indigenous impulses of nations. But this is not the only fatal fruit of this tree of good and evil. When men have once persuaded themselves that the promotion of their own interests is a convertible term for the general advancement of human happiness, it is easy to see through what channels human happiness will be advanced. When men once believe that to plunder the capital and absorb the industry of a sixth part of the human race, to whom they contribute neither capital nor industry, is but "the legitimate and necessary ascendency of the Christian west,"* it is almost a foregone conclusion what a rapacious and relentless despotism will spring from a hypocrisy so sordid and so cruel. And this is no mere occasional offence against the

---

* M. de Montalembert, p. 10.

rules of government; it is a deliberate conspiracy against the rights and liberties of mankind. It has been maintained and enforced at a cost of blood and treasure, and sin and misery, and ruined races and decimated generations, which will never be counted up till that day of reckoning when "British Christianity" and British government will be weighed in scales essentially "un-English." This inflexible imposture, which never drops its iron mask—which never reveals its inmost heart to man or God—which has made its language the vernacular of English politics and England herself the great Pharisee of nations, but which, under every disguise, is still self-interest and lust of rapine—this is the Unknown God of the English heart to which you have just offered up your devout *ex voto.* And this is the secret of your success. You have addressed your sympathy to the worst part of the Englishman's character, and you have done so at a time when men grasp at a straw for consolation. You have sounded the trumpet of his sordid despotism, you have sung the praises of his worst misdeeds, you have vindicated his vices and justified his crimes—all this he might have heeded not; but you have touched his cold heart and won his selfish sympathy by grovelling in the very dust in your worship of his weakness and his shame.

But you have done more, you have done worse. In taking your survey of English institutions in their general scope and particular operation, it could not have failed to strike you that there was one-third of the "great Christian nation" to which your felicitations did not wholly apply ; that this third was inhabited by men professing that component part of Christianity called the Catholic faith ; that Parliamentary government had not consulted their happiness quite as much as that of other parts, and that perhaps the constancy with which they adhered to their particular sect of Christianity might have something to do with their misgovernment. Any man with a spark of Catholic chivalry in his heart would have said something, were it only in a whisper, of the exceptional injustice which still distinguished the ecclesiastical institutions of Ireland. English self-conceit, however, is an exacting master, and if you had uttered a word of remonstrance against Irish misgovernment, you would have lost all the fame you had so dearly earned. Silence, therefore, under such circumstances, was a pitiable necessity, and might have been pitied in silence. But you were not satisfied with a silent sin. Having insulted the French clergy and their religious organs in order to propitiate the Protestantism of England—having insulted the Government and people of France, in order to flatter the national prejudice of England, as an act of final homage to that "great Christian nation whose institutions are more favourable to the propagation of Catholic truth and the dignity of the priesthood than any other regime under the sun,"* you turn by the wayside to where you see God's Church spoiled and usurped; "the dignity of the priesthood" spurned and dishonoured; "the propagation of Catholic truth" systematically trodden down by the very regime of which you have become the apostle; and you select that melancholy subject for gibes and reproach. I say, *you select*. You had bowed down in every point of the compass; you had worshipped Englishmen in every rank and station and profession and position—upper classes, middle classes, lower classes—in every act of their public or their private life, as legislators, as soldiers, as citizens, as sportsmen. Among all that host of men you *select*, as the sole and special objects of your obloquy, two Irish priests! No sophistry can cover the animus of this selection. Even if your allegations against them had been fairly stated, and had been reasonably pertinent to the matter at issue, the selection would have been more than suspicious; but they are stated with deliberate unfairness.

---

*M. de Montalembert.

John Haywood, Excelsior Steam Printing and Bookbinding Works, Hulme Hall Road, Manchester.

www.ingramcontent.com/pod-product-compliance
Lightning Source LLC
Chambersburg PA
CBHW020556270326
41927CB00006B/868